THE SLEEPING BEAUTY
& OTHER ESSAYS

BY THE SAME AUTHOR

Existentialism
The Seventh Solitude
Human Love: Existential and Mystical
The Path of Darkness
The World of the Thriller
The Existential Experience

THE
SLEEPING
BEAUTY

& OTHER
ESSAYS

RALPH   HARPER

International Standard Book No.: 0-936384-27-1
Library of Congress Catalog No.: 85-70174

"The View from Bujumbura" originally appeared in *Johns Hopkins Magazine*, March 1978; "The Concentric Circles of Loneliness" in *Humanitas*, November 1974; "The Weight of Our Time" in *Modern Age*, Winter 1985; "Walking to Maráthi" in *Queen's Quarterly*, Summer 1982; "Exercises from the Long Retreat" in *Cross Currents*, Summer 1983. Permission to reprint is gratefully acknowledged.

Cover design by James Madden, SSJE

Library of Congress Cataloging in Publication Data

Harper, Ralph, 1915–
    The sleeping beauty & other essays.

    Rev. ed. of: Nostalgia. 1966.
    Bibliography: p.
    1. Existentialsim.   2. Harper, Ralph, 1915–
I. Harper, Ralph, 1915–   . Nostalgia. II. Title.
III. Title: Sleeping beauty and other essays.
B819.H33 1985   142'.78   85-70174
ISBN 0-936384-27-1 (pbk.)

CONTENTS

Foreword by Richard Macksey

Essays

The Sleeping Beauty

I   Prologue

II   The Tale
1. Morning and Afternoon
2. Evening and Night
3. Before Dawn and Dawn
4. In the Fullness of Time

III   Epilogue

Notes

FOREWORD

Ralph Harper's enterprise resists easy definition. Unfortunately for our language, the word "meditation" has suffered an insidious erosion and sentimental cheapening since the seventeenth century, when it could evoke that intense, imaginative activity of poets and divines that challenged both the senses and the intellect. The very notion of "passionate thought" grounded in concreteness of imagery and experience makes the modern Anglo-American philosopher suspicious. Yet the literature of the self rests upon a succession of revolutionary meditative reflections, from Descartes to Husserl, essays that undertake to define a point of departure for a history of the consciousness.

Traditionally, meditation suggested an evolving personal exploration *toward* a certain topic but through a controlled situation or conceit, which invited the reader to participate actively in the experience. Ralph Harper's essay, "The Sleeping Beauty," is a meditation on the mysterious experience of *presence*, which guarantees the fidelity of fully apprehended reality and relationship but which can be evoked by the nostalgic longing that sometimes marks its very absence and refusal. Like Gabriel Marcel, Harper seeks a concrete approach to this experience through a "fundamental situation," here the Grimms' tale of Sleeping Beauty, the stages of her enchantment and recovery. Through the familiar narrative Mr. Harper leads us to discover a model for our passage in time, a voyage that traverses radical alienation from the world and the self but which has latent in its goal a genuine encounter in the fullness of time with reawakened presence. Like the tale, the essay describes a difficult journey through seemingly impassable obstacles to the recognition of what was all the while known and given. The journey described has the hermeneutic complexity of myth, a meaningful story of human destiny, and it demands of its readers that they elect the terms, immanent or transcendent, by which they will interpret it as a witness to their own life.

To recognize the "openness" of this fairy tale is not to deny the importance of its historical situation. It guards the entrance to an anguished moment in the human search for an identity and a name. It reflects a yearning for a transfigured reality separated from the conventions and rational certainties of society, and it conceals their emerging image of the last possible hero—as artist and exiled prince—a hero capable of action only in the distant past or prophetic future. The tale was governed by a new creative vision, which sought to translate the familiar into the wonderful. Nostalgia, in the profound solitude of the nocturnal tale, offered the only possible escape from the tyranny of impersonal time and faceless society.

Ralph Harper's essay illuminates the imaginative experience of many artists closer to our own time, writers who were transfixed by what Henry James calls "the Medusa face of life," but who still carried within their sensibilities the memory of another order, another possible relation that could redeem the "inconstancy, weariness, unrest" of an existence emptied of traditional values. Thus, in the search for "reconstructed" origins and "recuperated" life, in Proust's quest for Combray, in Kafka's probation before the Castle, or in Rilke's journey to the Prodigal's homeland, Mr. Harper discovers a dialectic between our contemporary anguish and that intense passion for existence that Jean Nabert called *l'affirmation originaire*.

Just as "The Sleeping Beauty" turns to the seminal literary texts of our time to make concrete the experience figured in the tale of the Sleeping Beauty, the essay also illuminates the reflections of many modern philosophers and theologians: Marcel, Lavelle, Max Picard, Mounier, Brunner, Buber, and Simone Weil. But the author also clarifies the choices and metaphors of Sartre, Jaspers, and Heidegger. He suggests that all modern ontologies can be comprehended within the original experience of nostalgia, for authentic being is first certified in its absence.

Ralph Harper's meditation on the stages in the journey to presence, as seen through the parabolic lens of this tale, is complementary to his book, *The Seventh Solitude*, on those great prophets and probationers of metaphysical exile—Kierkegaard, Dostoevsky, and Nietzsche. It was, in fact, Nietzsche's phrase for the profound homelessness and solitude of those who *renounced* "lost paradises" that gave Mr. Harper his title. That same solitude is here only a stage in the history of the Sleeping Beauty; after the promises and the blunted curse came the hundred-year's sleep, while the castle and its occupants were cut off from the world. The history of that outside world from which presence had been withdrawn and which seemed to doubt its very existence, has been, poignantly, our history as well. "The Sleeping Beauty" suggests, then, that the radical nihilism and exile afflicting our culture became the ground for that intense longing for being at the dark heart of much of nineteenth-century art and thought.

"The Sleeping Beauty" is not a tale for those seeking easy answers or handy categories. The tale that directs Mr. Harper's meditation must interrogate every reader; the author refuses to reduce it to simple allegory. It should be read as a *model* in which we can discover those successive aspects of separation, longing, and recognition within the temporal dimension of our own lives.

The five short, autobiographical essays that Ralph Harper collects for the first time in this volume add another, more personal dimension to the meditation recorded in the tale of the Sleeping Beauty. They are an itinerary of the imaginative landscapes, of the distances travelled, and of the places of a life remembered and examined. In terms of the last essay, they are exercises from the "Long Retreat"; building on memory and image, they are the "compositions of place" that we need to "restore a strong awareness of the immediacy of things." The landscapes evoked are old cities, Charleston, Oxford, Fribourg; the islands of the Cyclades and walking to the interior; spots in time on the great African continent, Bujumbura and Keur Moussa. Born a New Englander, Ralph Harper has travelled through many cultures and, as a meditative walker, explored many landscapes. In recent years he has made his home on a hillside in Maryland, but early and late the terrain he has explored is the complex interior life of the human imagination, the human journey.

Ralph Harper has remained incorrigibly a teacher. This has meant not only a testing of each novel or poem or essay or film he encounters, but a constant rereading and retrial of his own responses. It is to this perennial revision that his preoccupations and traditions commit him. As he observed in his most recent book, "The older I grow the more I come to respect the way experience forces me to review and revise. Impatient with other people's theories, I am constantly being disenchanted by my own."

The solitary walker of these essays is exploring and

revising his own favorite texts as well as the outposts of our fragmented culture. These records form a kind of *journal intime*, combining an immediacy of landscape and response with a self-interrogation that he finds in the achievements of literature and music and painting. The distance travelled and the space explored are defined in the always tentative terms of self-knowledge. The journey is triangulated by recognitions and separations—from Augustine (for whom the "unquiet heart" was a guarantee of an assurance lost to moderns) and from the tragic thinkers of the nineteenth century immured in their metaphysical solitude. It is also a record of miracles as well as losses, of the chemistry of memory and of losses recovered from extremity.

Writing in January 1900 when after a decade of silence John Ruskin had died, the young Marcel Proust grimly remarked that, with Nietzsche mad and Tolstoy and Ibsen at the end of their tethers, this death marked a turning-point. Europe was losing, one after another, its great "directeurs de conscience." Ralph Harper in his essays records similar senses of loss, but he also suggests how, paradoxically, Proust himself and another unlikely guide, Franz Kafka, have become in our time for a world transformed directors of conscience. Harper's circles of hours, days, and places recall the meditations of Proust; Kafka, in turn, bears for us the symbols of fear and failure that haunt our lives. Certainly no writer of our century has had a loftier sense of the vocation of literature than Kafka: as he wrote at nineteen, "A book must be the axe for the frozen sea within us." And it was Kafka who saw the impossibility of a literary homecoming. Writing to his editor in 1922, he confessed "the diabolical element" in writing. "It is vanity and lust for pleasure," he writes, "that constantly whirls around and enjoys one's own figure or else another . . . . The motion multiplies; it becomes a solar system of vanity." Ralph

Harper is fully aware of the claims of the literary imagination to liberate and redeem the reader, as well as its constant temptation to diabolical self-indulgence. For Harper it is Kafka who embodies the emblems of achievement and failure, the modern equivalents of Augustine's more confident *insecuritas*, rooted as it was in an older sense of sin. The predicament that Kafka enacts suggests one reason why these meditations are in a constant state of self-revision, but it suggests also why they are morally compelling.

The essays collected here move from Central Africa, "The View from Bujumbura," to West Africa, "Exercises from the Long Retreat." They form a vital gloss on the text of "The Sleeping Beauty." Like the texts of Proust and Kafka, they are never quite completed. They are an eloquent record of adjustments and recognitions, and exploration of the shifting frontiers that are the ghostly demarcations of our inner life.

Richard Macksey
Johns Hopkins University

ESSAYS

THE VIEW FROM BUJUMBURA
(Burundi: January 1977)

"We want you to do only what you want to do." A welcome
reversal of how I would speak to him when he was a child.
It was what I wanted to hear. For two weeks I would have
no responsibilities of any kind: no one I had to see, no
hospital visits, no church services, no school consultations,
no property or financial problems to arrange, no teaching,
nothing. I would enter a suspended life, letting myself be
fed, driven, entertained. I could not know that at the end
of a week, without internal warning, I would decide to walk
out the front door, and not stop walking until, two hours
later, I had walked past a hundred villas on the hill. From
that time on I became a fixture, twice a day, on the roads,
the only white man in Bujumbura who walked.

December 30—Our villa is on a hillside overlooking the city
and Lake Tanganyika. The view from the terrace, and from
my bedroom, reaches across the lake to the mountains of
Zaire. In the garden below are palms, avocados, frangi pani.
At night one sees the street lights and the lights from fishing
boats on the lake. The house is enclosed by a high wall and
is guarded night and day by two men. It once belonged to a
prince, the first prime minister. The present prime minister
lives just up the street; I can see the soldiers at his gate from
the bathroom. They stare at me when I walk past, and I am
afraid they may see to it that I too am asked to leave the
country. It is that kind of place. Downstairs in our house

1

visitors come and go, murmuring of Michelangelo. It is that kind of house.

Sometimes my son asks, "Do you want to come with me?" I usually do. One day it will be to see the World Health Organization director-general, a German who has worked in the South Seas and in Africa ever since the war. Another day it will be to the White Russian who manages a Belgian freight and travel office. We go one night to a Greek restaurant looking for someone who has just left. At sunset one evening we are sitting at the yacht club and the Egyptian ambassador joins us. The Zairois first secretary drops by—he is always dropping by. He says, "Bonjour, Papa." D. tells me to say, "Bonjour, Bébé." I never get the chance. He invites us to lunch in time. The Senegalese director of refugees comes to dinner. His wife is passing her bar degree by correspondence with Paris. We have dinner with an Italian who has built the only blacktop in the country. His wife is Danish. The other guests are Dutch, Algerian, French, Swiss. Another day we are out on the lake, and go alongside the Belgian ambassador and the French helicopter pilot. Every day I meet half a dozen new people from as many countries. I count up the number of nationalities working for the UN, 35. And there are as many working for themselves or for the government. No one stays longer than three years. There is hardly time to get tired of friends or hurt by gossip. This alone is vacation after the invariability of people at home.

December 31—In the late afternoon we go on a picnic in campers to the lower banks of the Rusizi River, a few miles above the point where it empties into the lake. It is almost dark when we drive out of the German soap factory yard and through the savannah beyond the airport. The dirt road winds among the brush and palms—I am reminded of Folly Island near Charleston 50 years ago. Each driver takes it fast to show his skill at missing potholes. Where we stop there is an open-sided thatched roof hut by the river. The men and children scatter to bring firewood in; the women unpack the food. I go off by myself to the edge of the brown stream, flowing so fast underneath the 15-foot sheer banks of grass. I say to myself with self-satisfaction, "This is Africa. I am in Africa." The Germans, with harmonica, sing "Lili Marlene"; I cannot remember my good old American songs, like "Old Kentucky Home." Our fire was being replied to 20 miles away in Zaire by a larger blaze. The air was very soft, and I walked over to the edge of the darkness and looked down into the mad river. When we got home the others went off to a New Year's Eve party, but I stayed home, fearful of being picked up after curfew by a jeep patrol.

January 1—Bernard, the cook, wanting to please me brings a bowl of mangos, papayas, and pineapple again for breakfast. He will do this for two weeks unless stopped. I do not like the bland local coffee and tea. I prefer the very powdered milk I forced D. to drink on our Maine island. Another reversal.

We skimmed down the lake in the Boston whaler. The hippos bobbed up to watch. Ours is the fastest boat on Lake Tanganyika, faster than the Burundi navy's Greek patrol boat. Natives pole long punt-like boats along the shore. They wave but do not want to be photographed. For that matter, neither would I. Others are leading their thin long-horned cattle to the edge of the lake to drink. When we beach the boat to swim, I walk through the tall grass towards the lagoon for shells; now I know where the chiefs got the impressive sea shells they used to wear around their necks. The lake is 20 miles across; over there was once a city of three hundred thousand, before the mercenaries and the UN

3

forces clashed. As we spin along the shore I observe that the hills—with high mountains beyond—are more sparsely treed and less inhabited than the hills in back of Bujumbura. There are no banana, coffee, and eucalyptus trees, no clusters of thatched-roof huts.

January 2—The nightmares have returned, the same sequence of the past two years. I am left badly shaken when I wake in the early morning. But through them I have come to understand something fundamental about my identity. We spend all day building and tying up a thing of straw and patches, and then when our hold loosens in sleep, the scarecrow falls apart and the soul crumples. My scenes recur, compositions of several places which I do not want to think about in the daytime. They become models for villages, schools, churches, homes at night: harbors, fields, mountains. The sky is always so low that it is as if there is no sun in that world, or almost dark. There are no people either, or else they are shadowy. My journeys must be taken on foot, and yet I traverse them quickly, and am able to see where I am going before I get there. Sometimes I try again and again to do something, and cannot. There is always a threat, and I am always afraid. My before-sleep strategies do not help me suppress or evade. Every point of my vulnerability, like an acupuncture point, is twisted and probed. I never have good dreams at all. In the daytime I am secure, finally, after 60 years. At night the security is gone: money, friends, jobs. I dream of standing before a congregation in my father's church, trying to keep them from talking or walking out on me. No good, they keep right on. I try at least to salve my professional sense by finding my place in a prayer book, any prayer book, and I can't. But when I wake up, so far I am always able to reconstruct my soul—what else can it be called—for another day. But I wonder sometimes whether the day will come when I will not have the resilience necessary.

January 3—I have never been so detached. I used to think I knew the several faces of solitude. Apparently not all. In this African country I am outside everyone. Everyone is black; I don't see the whites, I merely mention them in my journal. Whether from the car or from the road itself as I walk by faster than they, I overtake the single-file or two by two of cast-off shirts and trousers, draped prints from European mills. This is a silent country. No one shouts; perhaps no one dares to shout. The two tribes—tutsis and hutus—are wary of each other. For good reason: the hutus rebelled against the tutsis, several years ago, and the tutsis killed two hundred thousand of them. Both are watching and waiting for the next move. Everywhere there is a low murmur of voices, as in a doctor's stethoscope over the heart. At night absolute silence, as in death. Perhaps from inside their huts on the conical hills they listen for the soldiers in their green fatigues and black berets. And there are no lights except for the lights at the corners. In the thousands anywhere you drive they are walking, and carrying sticks and stones, water and food on their heads, bananas and firewood. If they have money, they pay to stand packed in the open backs of trucks. This country is said to have the highest density of people in all Africa, and yet it is difficult to believe it because there is so much green everywhere, green in an eroded land. And while they are not starving, most are undernourished, the land unreplenished, their diet without vitamins. The gross sight and smell of manioc root, their staple. Nothing is as it seems.

January 4—Things are getting sorted out. Memories of my own past which have become, as it were, mythic places, archetypal cities: Fribourg, Charleston, Paris. Two myths, not of my making, complement the scenes: Sleeping Beauty and the frog prince. Only memories which have not been spoiled either by hasty returns or failure have the right to form backgrounds for my leading stories. I am beginning to grasp something like the credibility of myself as a whole. I am a persistent undercurrent of expectation, fortified by memory. I must find other, new places with people where expectation can linger. Increasingly I want actualities of all sorts, even in film and fiction. I understand now my insistence on being able to look out a window when I study.

My old syndrome of discovery and breaking through: homesickness and the lost paradise. Journey to, not just from, paradise, returning in time and space, presence and absence, frustration, waiting, loneliness, being scared and depressed, to the openness of new relationships, the security of old, through anonymity to recognition, through incompleteness to some fulfillment. They all go with a complicated psychological phenomenon, so ambivalent in its pointing to my past while firing my future. Bittersweet, where lost dreams come true, places of salvation where one suffers for want of what we do not have. I have at times now a foretaste of total satisfaction. Is that a chimera?

There is nostalgia even in some nightmares. Is this why they ache? I used to think that nostalgia would replace depression. I know now that depression generally just lifts mysteriously sooner or later.

In the past two years my bodily energy has diminished because of angina, and as a result I have been able to understand the relevance of the frog prince myth. Instead of thinking of life as a waiting and wanting to break through to someone else, I have come to see my own as a wanting to break out of myself, my own mask and bonds. I am less pessimistic than before, because so much depends on me, that is, after I am hurled against the wall and shatter and am transformed to my original mold. Identity is to be released, not found.

January 5—We drove south 40 miles along the shore to Muronge. Beyond the capital the fields are flat and broad between the hills and the lake. They are subdivided into half-acre plots, each being cultivated with mattocks by women and children. On the hillside the huts are partly hidden by the banana trees. The road winds around the cliffs beyond the plain. There are fishing villages in coves, with nets and open boats with lanterns on the beach. Beyond the cliffs we drove through plantations of palm trees, laid out by the Germans before World War I. In the middle of one village a pole, as for a toll road, had been lowered over the road, to slow the traffic down (five trucks and three cars a day). We never saw Muronge itself, only a deserted so-called castle on the shore, the remains of the romanticism of a defrocked Belgian priest, murdered for his sodomy. It could become a motel some day. The beach there was white sand between rocks, as on Mt. Desert or Pelion. A brilliant Bar Harbor or Cycladean day, blue, gold, light wind. Only here a peninsula of Zaire loomed opposite.

Tonight I called on Prof. D., a Belgian law historian. We listened to Messiaen and talked of Oxford and Greece, places I too was happy in. I think of friends far away, Ruedi from Zurich and Fribourg, now dead, F. in Jamaica. I think also of a day here and there in other countries, walks in Copenhagen, an alpine pass in Norway. Every night I write a little before going to sleep. And then I turn out the light and lean on the casement and watch the lights moving on the lake, lights flickering on the Zaire shore miles away.

Jasmine and coppertone, honeysuckle and stone pines, in Fribourg and Fiesole, salt water marshes on the north shore, kelp, chemicals, and other spices, the red passenger ferry across Boston harbor and the narrow gauge on the other side, the steam whistle on the Boston and Maine to Intervale, pony cart and birches, a cry of fish and the clang of the trolley bells in Charleston, the old "Sappho" to Sullivan's Island, scillas, wistaria, and hanging moss, the ramparts of Fribourg and Gotteron, Gothic fountains and tumbled stony stairs, the baroque Eglise St. Michel, the Hofgarten and Hofkirche in Innsbruck, an army band trying to play the Horst Wessel song and walk at the same time (I laughed so hard my friends had to pull me away). It is all mixed up inside, all this and much more, the stuff of those who write poetry not philosophy. I know I cannot be understood—even by myself—without it, fireflies and crickets, juniper and thyme. If I had to draw heaven, it would contain all this.

January 6—I walked down the hill to the city (a term of courtesy). After an hour I am very tired from walking in the sun, and sit in the cool of the Embassy entresol. I am too tired to talk to D.'s colleagues as they pass. In the market next door each peddler has staked out a few feet on the bare earth, one for nails and screws, one for toothpaste, another for fish, and so on. It is the only place where there is noise and disorder, a safety valve for the revolutionary council. Knowing their history I am astonished at their composure. From Germans to Belgians to independence, from kings and princes to presidents and prime ministers, from tribes to massacres. One day foreigners are welcome, the next day they are escorted to the airport, stripped, searched and packed off. One day for themselves tranquillity, the next torture and killing. They do not speak to us; they do not speak to each other either. They are the most secretive people on the continent.

For me it is a blessing, to be totally non-attached, non-aligned, for a while. I can escape the acceleration of noise and energy that Henry Adams worried so much about, the vast unsorted data and processing machine that is America, that unsafe, sick, and saddened comfort station. At home when I have forced myself to think about what I am surrounded by, the layers and buffeting of facts, demands, and changes, my head goes round and I sigh, "No more, no more." Mind out of focus, slap-slapping me with past and present mixed, a moan of feeling that life should be simpler than this and still be true. I have illusions of control. Death is controlled—held back—sickness is controlled—held back—poverty is under control—held at bay. I have them now where I want them. And then a nightmare says, "The hell you have."

January 7—Oh, to be a banana tree. When the fruit is picked, it withers, but then it grows again. On this side of death we ebb and drain, tidal rhythms, troughs and waves, crests and breakers, manic-depressives, suppressed writhings. This does not mean I forget that life is for the most part a marking-time, even worse than standing-still. Restlessness is hard to live with. Oh, to be a sea anemone, opening and shutting, waiting for attention in clear rock pools, then closing before one gets hurt. Life is not an adventure that has failed so much as an adventure that has hardly begun.

I have said that I am not adventurous and have had no adventures. And yet what after all is an adventure? A spin-off, eccentric, often unnoticed because it does not fit preconceived pictures of heroic flourishes. I have said I do not need people. I forget my dependence on teaching, new faces, voices, the rise and roll of unimagined ideas and arguments. I have said I have no identity problem. Why then do I have such unsettling dreams? Plainly I do not know myself at all, or else I lie.

We walked into the Cercle Sportif after dark, casing the joint. Three black men were seated at a table drinking. They stopped talking as we approached, and waited for D. to speak first. Each of them had done some terrible thing during the rebellion. Now they are at ease, they use the polite words that civilized men use. It is that kind of country. It is that kind of world too. At the gate the guards wear blankets and carry spears.

I too use civilized words. Underneath, the mistrust of self and others is pretty strong. I was brought up on the language of St. Paul, but I do not share his concepts. He could disown, disclaim boasting of self because he really knew he had someone better to boast of. If we disown ourselves, we fear there will be nothing left to claim. We get caught coming and going. In boast I say that I am self-disciplined, that I can and do make my body and my mind—feelings are another matter—do what I tell them. But there's the trick. I underline the discipline of body and mind, and am overturned by my feelings. I say—and I like to hear others say—I am honest with myself and others. And it is true, within limits. Always an exception to the self-praise. I am responsible in many directions. After all, I do many things. But they are routines and duties, not beloved obligations to which I am called. Without them I might levitate, like St. Teresa of Avila in her choir. Apart from routines set there seems to be no guarantee of stability. I have reason enough not to trust my tarnished self-image further. Another reason why it is good to get away from places where I am in the habit of displaying it.

I should speak maybe of things not done, rather than of places visited and ideas found. Opportunities missed, like spending a weekend with William Temple at York or meeting

Graham Greene at Campion Hall or cruising with R. G. Collingwood in the Aegean or walking with John Buchan at Elsfield, even teaching in Minnesota or Ohio instead of sitting on my ass at Harvard waiting for a chair and an honorary degree. Out of such inertia and conceit I have learned that Camus was right when he said, "Nothing is true that forces one to exclude." I now ask two questions. What have I omitted? And what is it really all about?

January 8—I cannot quite understand how people can bring themselves to talk at length to psychiatrists, exposing themselves without recall and pasting over. There is a better way. I know Kafka and Proust almost as well as I know myself. I encourage them to talk instead of talking myself. My students and I play the game of patient and psychiatrist with them instead of with ourselves. It works pretty well; no one goes away embarrassed or ashamed. In teaching there is a nice combination and balance of detachment and confession, analysis and commitment. The trick is to have some system—preferably several—to use as a sounding board. Even Socrates had that. Even?

When they were out tonight the lights went out, only on the hill, not in the city. It has happened each time we showed a movie. Tonight I wanted to read. I could not find flashlight or candles. I had to think instead. When I was a boy an English clergyman at a church conference said that a test of a person is to make him sit in an empty country railway station on a rainy day for several hours. Even then I did not think that much of a test. I have always thought life like an empty railway station. Like Thomas Buddenbrook I was brought up on the seacoast, and liked to listen to the surf. I was accustomed to heavy New England snows, and blackouts from primitive power systems. Silence and darkness are both familiar. Their blankets are my security. I am not indifferent, however, to indifference or hostility. I shudder at the labileness of fidelity. And I would like to believe that only those who are pre-occupied with some central struggle have strength enough to sustain fidelity to others or give it consistently in return.

In my country—only rarely do I acknowledge my possessing and being possessed by a country—in my country, I say, the faithful often seem to be the same as the losers. "Blessed are the losers," F. said, "for they see God." That is clever, but I do not believe it. I am not sure I want to believe it either; I'd rather win. I have not attained that plateau of purity, of detachment, that both religion and philosophy advocate. I am a man with and part of a country, spiritually thin and unjustifiably assertive. A winner takes all culture, built on fear of failure, bleeding for recognition and rewards. If one rejects any of the mutual acceptance societies that are available for everyone, life is a pretty lonely business. They are surrogates for winning. In the end it feels the same. Our greatest panic is to end life in a hospital bed unvisited, forgotten. I dreamed that last night. So how in all honesty can I say "Blessed are the losers"? They don't see God, they see nothing. Of course, I know an answer. They don't see, but they are, something, and that above all matters. The trouble is that is not what matters in my country, and I cannot seem, after ignoring it for so long, to separate myself from time and place. That is why we are a sad people whose occasional sophistication is not redemptive.

Everywhere I live among people with secrets. They peer out of bus windows, embarrassed to see my eye on them. The black schoolgirls giggling as they walk past on their way to the lycée have their secrets as I have mine. The revolutionary council has secrets from the country, and we foreigners have some too or we would not be here. We want what we dare not admit, we have done what we don't want someone else to know, we fear what we hardly dare confess, even to our heart of hearts. Secrets tell us more about ourselves than true confessions—for who can tell enough truth to convince anyone for long? No wonder our day is the day after the night of espionage.

January 9—We picked up our friend the Rumanian geologist this morning. We were driving to northern Burundi near the Rwanda border. He had explored that area for uranium and knew it well. The road, black-top all the way, wound up from the plain, higher and higher, up to six thousand feet, and cold. We drove fast, and marveled at the miles of women walking down to Sunday market. The walls of the cuttings were red laterite. "Where's the uranium?" "There, everywhere, waiting for investments to pay for the processing." Finally we turned off onto a narrow dirt road which led to the mission church at Katara. Cathedral size, brick, low roof, long enough for the thousand people standing for mass inside. Hundreds of others were standing on the terraced steps, and as we parked we heard singing from within. Except for the White Father facing us at the altar all were black. For the first time in years I felt at home. I knew what all this was about. When a basket of bread reached me in the back, I took a piece and held my tears in hard. I too am human, and these are my brethren. The drums led the singing. Everyone but me knows the words. It doesn't matter. I know what it is all about.

Afterwards the Belgian priest gives us coffee and describes the life of the mission: the division of the parish into hills, the reading program to the end that the baptized can read the Gospel and understand their new life, the community's care of the sick and the poor. It is a religion even a communist can respect; it is communism. We drive on to the next church where a mass is also taking place. I

13

stand behind the altar this time, with the choir led by a teenager in an alb. And afterwards the French Canadian priest continues their story.

We drive as far as the Rwanda customs post and picnic beside a mountain stream, watched by a gaggle of laughing little boys. On the return we stop at the White Fathers' language school at Kayanza. I ask how long it takes to learn the language. "You can never learn it well enough to preach in it. I read my sermons which I have had translated for me each Sunday." And yet he has lived in Burundi 20 years, and with others has compiled its first dictionary. "It is a complicated language, five tones and 50 thousand words. They are a complicated people." A few miles away there is a Chinese labor camp. As we pass a group of them out walking, we wave, and just as the Burundi children wave back and smile, so do the Chinese. Who are the uncomplicated ones in this fine world?

I am thinking now of the world I think I know that I will be going home to soon. It overlaps already with this one here. I know how lucky they are at Katara to make the transition from tribal life to Christian life, real Christian life, not the life of churches I know. How long will they be allowed to stay there? In America we are far from that now, so far it is hard to speak of it except in overblown terms, like "final struggle," "apocalypse." I remind myself to smile. But I do suppose at times—and I cannot escape the rhetorical completely—that it is not the right to be private that we should protect so much as the possibility to be oneself that we must define. It is a lot harder to take our national and racial institutions seriously now than in my father's time. They have been identified with such shoddy men in recent years. We hesitate to salute institutions at all, let alone with respect. We don't live in a country where saluting means much any more. What many generations of

14

patriots and missionaries contrived and lived by now seems trivial and unworkable, even where it is not poisoned by grabby men. We do not look beyond ourselves to gods or symbols purer than ourselves. The little gods are made in our image. It is doubtful that there are 36 just men left. This morning I had a view of the world as it might have been, a vision I learned many years ago and that makes me feel guilty once in a while. Tomorrow I prepare to return to a different world. Is there time left for the comedy of losers who are really content to be left alone?

I am impressed by the UN specialists that I have met. They have an openness, humor, and dedication that is not politically motivated, and that seeks moderate personal awards. And yet in most countries, as here, they are on sufferance, and soon become disillusioned and glad when their tour is over and they can go back to the world of private gain. Altruism doesn't last long without encouragement.

January 10—We go out in the boat for the last time. I neither swim nor ski, but I can steer and enjoy D.'s grace. I say, "Perhaps next year I will be stronger." But I know that D. will not be here next year, nor will I. His house which seemed his home will be someone else's. I find this kind of fact hard to get used to. Nor will I walk up into the hills again before supper, never. This morning, in between ski runs, we stopped in the middle of the lake and talked. Last week when Alexey, the Soviet counselor, came with us, we stopped and talked too. But that was not the same. He invited himself, and that was unusual, but the questioning on both sides, though good-humored, was wary. It has taken 35 years for this father and son to talk, and there was no torrent, only a few careful sentences. I wanted to know what he wanted to do with his life, how he saw it. He told me. It was like the good times in a class when someone is trying to explain a text or an author, and ends by explaining himself. The result is a circle of quiet around the speaker.

January 11—Each afternoon I have walked a little farther on the road winding up beyond the boys' school. They greet me with "Yambo," and I say "Yambo" in reply. It is my only word, but it helps me on the way. They are not accustomed to being spoken to at all by whites. A little girl descends from a spring with an open bowl of water on her head, not a ripple. I do not look too directly at the women, and speak only to the elderly. The old men are always respectful, and I of them. I can imagine this road to the interior going on and on, a hundred miles or more to Tanzania, and then on to the Indian Ocean. I have never felt such an urge to keep on walking. Around each bend there is always something new. It is the way life should be. Today at dusk we drove up the same road, but several miles beyond the farthest bend I had walked, to a toy house with a turret. We sat on the terrace in the sunset and waited for the headlights of our Hungarian host, appearing and disappearing on the road. Neither the lake nor Zaire seemed any farther off than from my bedroom miles below. The generator was not working, and we ate bread, cheese, and sausage, and drank red wine in the light of kerosene lamps and candles. Another link between Bujumbura and Maine.

January 12—On the plane to Nairobi, Dr. K., returning to Munich on business, said, "There is something special about going to Africa. I never get tired of it." He had lived there over 20 years, I had been in Africa only two weeks, and I felt the same. It is not like remembering Greece, that landscape of paradise. Paradise is more exhilarating. But just as everyone should catch a glimpse of paradise, if he can, so everyone should be given a suspended sentence in Africa before his passage down the slide becomes too fast to be stopped. I had badly needed to put some distance between myself and my commitments. What I saw from Bujumbura had that effect.

With six hours to wait in the Brussels airport, a gray, cold winter morning, I sat the whole time in the vast transit lounge, and thought of this time and this place as another buffer between me and the camouflaged fears and failures of each day. When I got home and settled in, to my surprise I felt no jet lag for the first time. It was as if I had been able to bring an eternal time back and apply it to the time I had left behind when I traveled to a land where time itself began.

THE CONCENTRIC CIRCLES OF LONELINESS

I have been thinking about loneliness all my life, long before I wrote *The Seventh Solitude: Metaphysical Homelessness in Kierkegaard, Dostoevsky, and Nietzsche* (ten years ago). I was not an orphan. I was brought up by parents who loved me and who did not die until I myself was married and had children. I have had close friends, and others whom I respect and who have liked me. I have no excuse to be an authority on natural or social loneliness.

I was brought up within a Christian (Episcopalian) family, in a rectory. From childhood I was always interested in church and religion. There was never a time, even for a period of ten years when I stayed away from church-going, when I lost interest in theology, and in what Tillich was to call "the method of correlation" (which no longer makes sense to me).

In college I went through a kind of religious conversion, partly out of social loneliness, and partly as a result of my reading of Unamuno, Kierkegaard, Augustine, Newman, Barth, and Aquinas, and my introduction quite by chance to the Roman Mass. For a few years I actually became a Roman Catholic. At that time I was fortunate to be able to know that denomination at its best, not only by living for months in a Benedictine priory but for two years in a Jesuit House of Studies at Oxford under Martin D'Arcy. In that period I had many long conversations with Dominican fathers both at Oxford and Fribourg, and was lucky enough to have conversed on a personal level with Etienne Gilson and Ronald Knox. I never experienced the totalitarian side of Catholi-

18

cism. My fading away was even more by chance than my conversion, and without pain. I know from within, however, what it is to be programmed to believe and to try to believe. I feel I have been de-programmed for some years now.

For one who like me has spent so much of his life thinking about and writing about the relationship between religion and existential experience—just call it experience—it is important, I think, not to hide the literary and reflective background representing not only a social tradition out of which I have grown, but the later efforts I made to understand, as well as one can from outside, both Eastern Orthodoxy—I once lived in Greece—and the older and still viable forms of non-Christian Eastern religion and thought, from Hinduism and Buddhism to Sufism.

It has taken me much longer probably than for others to be able to stand outside all this, in part because something inside me—programmed or not—has wanted to accept something of what mankind has reached for in answer to the conflicts and dread of existence, and partly because I have enormous respect for systematic understanding of any kind. But in the end I found myself, not only no longer able to pray, but no longer able to swallow my own hope that I was simply passing through a typical "dark night of the soul." In brief, I found I was standing outside myself as well, at least outside a self that so far as I could understand it, had always existed side by side with a consistent intellectual and emotional make-up and drive which has guaranteed whatever uniqueness and integrity I possess.

The time came when I could no longer repeat with feeling Ingmar Bergman's knight's cry, "Why can't I kill God within me?" and mean by that that the final loneliness of man is to fear that he must live without God. That fear has disappeared along with the cry, and I fear now only separation from certain people, a separation almost as certain as the quasi-absolute certainty that there is no God to be separated from in life or death. I see clearly today that in all my writing—seven books to date—I have consistently struggled to express a nostalgia reaching beyond the depressions and tragedies of life to an assurance of affection and understanding fidelity that seem to me the only ultimate ideals of human existence. If I have been doggedly ruthless in outlining this underlying program of my mind, I have been equally ruthless in settling for nothing that does not live up to my sense of what is possible.

And so when I now say that I am, in some way, on my own, I am saying two things: first, that at last I have been able to separate what I live by (I do not mean what I make a living doing—that is a more complicated, but not I think an inconsistent part of the story) and what I have always been in heart and imagination and tentative reflection. Where I once tried to integrate (as in a "method of correlation") what I had received with what I found, I now unemotionally can retract a line from the closing pages of my first—and unreadable—book, "the believer is to be envied." I do not envy believers in invisible counterparts of what experience alone, for me, validates. The world alone is all I can believe in, with its insecurities and its unexpected joys.

This makes it very difficult, of course, for me to return to the kind of discussion of "metaphysical solitude" which I am, in a small way, even now a specialist in. I still teach Dostoevsky and Nietzsche—and most of the others I have written about—and I still expose their obsession with the death of God (and all the changes that can be rung on that phrase, from then to now). They cannot be understood without our understanding what it meant to them, in cultural and personal terms. Kierkegaard is another story. I would now refer to his solitude as psychological isolation— experienced also by Dostoevsky and Nietzsche but not central to our understanding of them. Kierkegaard believed passionately in God from beginning to end, even though in some strange way he affected to hold back from the absolution he felt he needed above all else, an absolution that would have relieved his "self-isolation." He had, to use his own image, locked himself in a room and thrown the key away. The only reasonable explanation that I can give for this is to say that he was born that way. I feel much the same—and am not embarrassed by the simplicity of my conclusions any more—about Dostoevsky and Nietzsche. The former may have been the first to relate sadism and masochism to the rootlessness of modern man without God, but I do not see that this explains his temperamental obsession with sadism and masochism. The man who has told us that all contradictions can exist side by side, and that we can and can want to do the worst to ourselves and others, knowing full well what the best is and loving that best, is also a man who had locked himself in a room and thrown away his key.

When we consider Nietzsche—for whom I have warm feelings—I cannot avoid feeling that he, unlike the other two, was a creature of pathos. He really did seem to want friends. He did not want to live totally imprisoned and isolated, however much he touted the necessity for an artist-philosopher of solitude, even the seventh and last solitude. Without God or friends, his mind struggled to achieve the beginning of a new evaluation of the theoretical basis of civilization, depending on nothing already received and tried out. He wanted understanding, and he failed to get it. He probably wanted affection as well, but it is hard to get one without the other. So much in life depends on chance meetings, and whether the peculiar mix of interest and character and priority of values can make or break or just plain alleviate the vulnerability independent minds suffer from. We do so often set up barriers that we hope others will knock down for us. The more gifted, the thornier, the more we even resist their efforts, and we are at times our worst enemies and most persistent mourners. There is a mystery in us all as to why we turn out one way or another, why we cannot accept or reach the only paradise worth losing. Much depends on chance, obstinacy, small-mindedness, self-centeredness, previous and unexamined commitments, in short, on the stubbornness of both fact and the unforeseen. The history of ideas hardly accounts for the history of persons.

"I think continually of those who are truly great" (Stephen Spender), or at least I used to, and I cannot curtail this level of discussion of loneliness without mentioning Proust and Kafka. I do not think of Proust as a lonely man. The major effort of his life and career was a search for his own lost time. But it ended not in the literary success we all know and admire, the demonstration of a creative, a fictional memory founded on involuntary, associative memory, but rather on the illusion—that is utterly foreign to me—that all is not lost when all is lost. That seems to me to place a sign of desperate lie and pathos over his name more unhappily pronounced than the pathos of Nietzsche, who wanted friends (Proust had many friends, devoted to him), but lived in a hermitage, now here now there, from which he never emerged except to be rescued for the smaller darkness of insanity, cared for by relatives who did their best to distort his meaning.

As for Kafka, whom I find it impossible to think about except in terms of amused affection—a man I know I would have liked, as his many friends did—if there was anyone who was convinced that he was more utterly condemned to outer darkness I have not come across him. Again, perhaps he could not help it; perhaps it was his father's fault after all—

who knows—and again, perhaps, as he often said to his long-suffering fiancée, Felice Bauer, the only thing he cared about was his writing. The single impression that I have taken away from years of reading and teaching him with sympathy is of a man lost in a labyrinth in the center of which sits a holy grail of inimical nothingness. What can make a man feel more estranged from life than that?

It is all very misleading. I have come to think that one spends so much time—I have, at any rate—thinking about the truly great that we forget the forms of loneliness—call it what you will, isolation, estrangement, alienation—and solitude, that almost everyone one knows has some direct experience of, and a good deal more that is visually indirect. You do not have to be a kind of pastor and teacher like myself to know the whole sad story of the sense of being left out, indeed, of being left out and behind as other lives move within their own commitments. I often wonder whether, in the first place, there really are experiences that mankind has not had until certain times in history, and whether our present obsession—not too strong a word—with loneliness (even the crowd can be lonely, we are told) may not be a phenomenon of the history of the present century, whatever its nineteenth century foreshadowings. I just do not know. After all, there have always been refugees and homeless ones, even though we seem to have spawned more in my lifetime than ever before (but perhaps even that is not true, except in relative, statistical terms). There have always been orphans. There have always been parents who have lost children and close friends and lovers. There is always the time when one of us dies before or after those his whole world was built on, and we are now alone without the sustaining meaning of love or care. This is to me ultimate loneliness, not the death of God—who at best seems to have been a wager of the imagination, however convincing the circles of trust in his invisible friendship and reported promises.

Perhaps it is a prudent and safer beginning to recall something Gabriel Marcel often said, that our world seems to encourage betrayal. Of all the forms of solitude, the worst—I would call it the eighth, the innermost center of the other seven circles—is the state of mind of one who having trusted someone, finds himself unmistakeably disappointed and let down. It is the fear of this that stirs waters of panic in premonitory waves more often than we are clearly conscious of. The loss of confidence in public leaders, the displacements and disillusionment that follow, is small beer to the discovery that someone you bet your life on, you did not know well enough after all. The sudden and unstoppably widening crevice that appears between man and woman (or for that matter, between any two persons, young or old) can be devastating if the experience of trust had been the absolute (the only absolute) center of one's existence.

So much of each week is sapped by expectations becoming wisps, frustrations galore, sheer plodding and eroding fatigue, the tempering of belief in change for the better, that to construct a life—or better said—to have been handed gratuitously a construction that promises a new life, built on respect, affection, trust, is the human equivalent of the mystic's substitution for us exiled children of Eve of a heart and land where all trouble is sorted out and comfort permanently released.

If estrangement is our lot and reconciliation—whatever you call it—our goal, how terrible it is to accept proof that what looked like our only chance for recognition has been withdrawn or had been an illusion all along. Fortunately, most people either never—so far as I can tell—come very close to this naked terror and void, or have different kinds of physical and social insurance to enable them to shut their eyes in time and walk away from this precipice. It is extraordinary how clever human beings are in taking and taking part in the preventive measures that save us from ourselves, save us from the eighth solitude. It takes a combination of bad luck—and bad picking—and a special concentration of vision for one to look the naked terror in the face and survive.

I am convinced that what one can see in those moments of awful vision is the poor, bare forked animal that is the original fact of existence, the flesh that the fourth Gospel claims the Word became. Until we understand the poverty of this first and last loneliness, we will never even begin to understand the point and possibility of it all making some sense (of flesh rising to the Word). The greatest things, no doubt, may be the simplest, but they are usually the ones that are too painful—or so we fear—to take in, and consequently we may find ourselves retracting much of what we thought and said, for the sake of what at the moment seems truer, makes more sense of what is happening, and doing the very opposite of what Wittgenstein recommended, namely, reducing both the complexity and simplicity of theory and conviction to guesses that we can more honestly live with. The justification for this kind of reduction—which may well march side by side with an intensified awareness of final loneliness—is actually the same one that prompted Wittgenstein to warn against contempt for the individual instance, and above all, individuals whom we love, at the top of our list of priorities.

A list is one thing and individuals something else. Moreover, one has no business blaming others all the time for breakdowns of trust. It takes more than the character and behavior of one or both partners in a game of trust to either guarantee or destroy the dreamed of and discovered foundation of hope. It takes determination never to give up one more tentative touch and question. Can this be counted on? Who can tell? Here again, there is a mystery of personal resource and strength that neither reason nor experience can always be counted on to mine and manufacture. Miracles keep occurring, and so do losses. To lose another person is tantamount to losing oneself. What gives us reason to go on living when we know what can happen to bring us back to our original solitude is some demonstration that loneliness is not only relieved according to dearest and longest dreams, but may be transformed in ways beyond imagining.

THE WEIGHT OF OUR TIME

In 1959 I wrote an essay on Augustine and Proust. In it I said, "Any comparison of two such different men raises a serious question of the motive behind the comparison. One can only say that such a juxtaposition is also part of an interior dialogue within the person doing the comparing." For me at that time Augustine and Proust were the two poles of my being, not just my thinking. They represented a real tension between ideal and reality. This tension was attractive because the two men had important themes in common: memory, time, love, and a quest for the fullness of the self. It was an example of an existential dialectic, and the changes it rang reverberated in my writing, my teaching, and my life.

Now, in 1981, having lived from the first quarter of the twentieth century to the last quarter, I see that something has changed, not only in me, but also in the possibility of understanding and commitment in our time. I have come to suspect that it is not possible to escape a measure of historical determination of one's deepest preconceptions and convictions. I no longer feel about Augustine as I once did. What was central to him no longer remains as lively an option for me; whatever tension I now hold in place, Augustine's position is not an important element of it. This would be easy to account for if I were expressing some personal crisis of belief. I am not. I have come to this pass from another direction altogether. In the past ten years, both in teaching and writing, I have found myself observing again and again that there seem to be themes that are important now which were not important to people of the nineteenth century, or to those of us brought up on nineteenth century premises, themes like identity, failure, nostalgia, insecurity. These are themes of our time, and they weigh on us as heavily as God, sin, praise, disquietude once did. The change is evidence of a movement within history which the feeling, thinking individual cannot really stand aside from today. I had once thought I could. But as I became interested in these themes and noticed that they were to be found in the literature of our time, it became increasingly difficult to remain in touch with the older themes. It was easier to be moved by problems of identity than by problems of God, by failure than by sin, nostalgia than praise or adoration, insecurity than disquietude. The differences were qualitative. I had become limited, if not impoverished, by them.

Take Augustine's exhilarating lines, "My love is my weight," and "Our hearts are restless until they rest in You." A promise is implied. If you follow your restlessness or love to the end, you will reach God. You cannot miss. Like Augustine you can always wander and make false moves before you get to the end, but there is an end and you can reach it. "You were within me, and I was outside." This is the fundamental Augustinian dialectic and optimism. The difference today is that we do not seem to get to that end— or any end, for that matter—and no longer care. What seemed so real to Augustine is apt to appear abstract to us, and, therefore, irrelevant. In 1959 I could feel the magnetism of soaring towards God, the heroic humility, the praise of lovers of God whose poetry shone brighter than all others. They are no longer with us except in books, and I find it difficult to imagine, with my late twentieth century mind, what conditions in the future might make them live again.

I recognize the role of history in this. I look back to the first quarter of this century, to the time of manifestos, to

Rathenau, Jaspers, Berdyaev, Marinetti, Ortega, Le Corbusier, Spengler. They may have been faulty prophets, but they and their readers felt they could read the future in the present. We do not. The change is a deprivation. For when the human spirit loses confidence in the future and struggles with the present alone, an element is missing that is needed to challenge intellect. When sin becomes the guilt of failure, withdrawal from belief in the possibility of the God-relationship to total self-centeredness represents the loss of a dimension in human nature.

There is no lack of talk about God. But can one really compare the God-talk of fundamentalists—self-centered, politicized—with the God of Eckhart, Mechthild of Magdeburg, St. John of the Cross? Can one ever confuse the self-consciousness of encounter groups and the gregariousness of parish programs with monastic discipline and fervor? We can remember how universal were the private daily prayers before the Blessed Sacrament. Now we are the relics, as we experience the actualities of Nietzsche's terrible prophecy.

> "You will never pray again, never adore again, never again rest in endless trust . . . no resting place open to the heart where it has only to find and no longer to seek."

Once the goal was faith, now it is self-confidence.

There is no lack of talk about guilt, but it is apt to take the form of denial. It is not just that excuses are easily found for malice and evil-doing, but that everyone is so afraid of acknowledging superior virtue, let alone a superior being. We are left with ourselves, and that is a very lonely state. When judgment disappears, so does the possibility of redemption. Instead of sin and real guilt, we speak of what we feel—failure to please others, failure to reach our own goals. Human beings did not always overrate money and success to the point of being totally defined by them and by the temporary and shoddy models of success. I am defined by what others say of me, not by what I am and have done. When others remain silent, I stop existing. The world is made up of winners and losers, mostly losers. Life is for this reason—more than because of our mortality—labile. There is no assurance any of us can become or remain a winner. Nerves are shot trying to play this new game. There was a time when we could be content with trying to compare ourselves to accepted heroic figures from the past, and above all others, Christ. Conformity to the present has replaced the self-discipline required by spiritual exercises.

There is no lack of attention to celebrities, but it would be silly to confuse this with the praise of greatness. Celebrities are forgotten almost as soon as they appear. The truly great are often not known at all. So little in modern education even tries to bring them to our attention. We are obsessed with using transient brightness to distract ourselves from pressures around us and our own dullness. At best, we are left with a kind of nostalgia for what might be. No century has used so much of its time marking time, doing busy work, because both past and future are so dim. No wonder there is no belief in conversions and visions of what life is all about. Augustine and we belong to different worlds, and there is no space shuttle to transport us in between.

There is no dearth of talk about freedom, especially freedom to choose. But the choices are themselves practical ones, not ends. But even here, unless I am mistaken, freedom of choice is not what moves the soul of middle-class America. Rather we are preoccupied with insecurity. We do not want to be free, but to be safe. The freedom we take for granted—unexercised—is a far cry from the liberation of the matter-bound, twisted soul of Augustine. He had exercised all his options and discovered that what he needed most was to leave the two-dimensional world of ideas and desires which had become his desert and his trap. His conversion was discovery that there was nothing left but to let self go and listen. He then heard the God of his heart, the God that had so little in common with the God of his seeking. This we, with our time-wasting essays on "Does God Exist?" have not understood very well. So long as Augustine thought of rest as the terminus to his search for identity—what he came to call his search for God—there was to be no rest. The actual end of his seeking came about when he realized in exasperation that what he needed was to put his moral house in order.

If there is a point where Augustine and we meet, it might be in our use of the word, insecurity. But the differences are large. Not only did he understand disquietude to be a built-in guarantee of a happy end to striving, he would have recognized that we are preoccupied with a different burden, fear of external forces. How curious it is that in the age of the Vandal, Augustine's insecurity was determined by the vortex of personal desire, not social and political menace. Unlike Kafka, who might be said to have carried for us the symbols of our fear and failure, Augustine experienced the frustration of one who has done everything, thought everything, and ended tied up in knots of his own making. Perhaps if Kafka had been able to break down and weep like Augustine, he too would have been released.

Liberation is not, however, the mark of the human. Camus said, "Nostalgia is the mark of the human." For us, it may be. For Augustine, it was praise. Nostalgia needs only a longing heart; praise needs one worthy of praise. The difference is one of dimensions; Augustine had one more than we. He sinned, we fail; we want to be safe, he wanted to be free; we desire, he praised. His human being was "a great

31

deep"; ours is an inner world of fish scurrying about on the face of that deep.

I think the present situation is actually worse. There is no mystery like the mystery implied by the profundity of the interior life, but that seems to be denied us. We know what we fear; acceleration (Henry Adams), manyness (Ortega), violence (Fanon), and banal evil (Arendt). I lived abroad between 1937 and 1941, and yet it has taken forty years for the moral enormity of the Nazi death camps to sink in. Over and over I ask myself how I would have behaved, and I am uneasy with the possible answers. I have been able to take for granted most of my life a stability underwritten by good health, an adequate intelligence, a supportive family, a first-rate education, a variety of things to do, travel and financial security. I have never been tested as millions of our contemporaries have, let alone tortured, deprived, exiled. On the other hand, I have lived as they would like to live, and have had time to sort things out, as they have not. I have had time to practice the disciplines of thought and behavior that keep the worst nightmares at bay. It is easy for me to understand Kafka and Proust; they were middle-class, like me.

We spend too much time avoiding distractions, even religious ones, so that we can recover a sense of what it is to be human. We know the avenues of escape, we know roles and functions, far better than we know what kind of life is worth living and worth praising. I am troubled by the constant pressure to take in everything that comes to my attention, so much more than any computer but God can handle. I am distracted by desires and ideas like everyone else, and distracted as well by the routines I have developed to make time until I have sorted out enough to make myself believe I am getting somewhere. Instead of seeking a reprieve from intolerable pressures, I try for an equilibrium made

32

possible by having learned painfully what does not work. This may be the only wisdom of old age now possible. I would like to think that even though my nerves may be just as vulnerable as when I was younger, the time of critical danger has passed. But is equilibrium everything?

The Pascalian equation of lost God—lost man may be our equation. There is no continuing city. Perhaps there never was. In its place there could be a new foundation for charity itself, in our privacy. This is paradoxical, but possibly true. Privacy, unlike charity, has always been possible. You can inhibit but you cannot crush it, as long as self-discipline lives; only the self itself can reject it. The question is, what are we to do with privacy. That must be answered if we are to promote it seriously. I have a suggestion. Why not find some Platonic ideas for the reality we already know and fear the loss of? When I first read Plato, it seemed obvious to me that Plato had got it wrong. The world we experience is the only one, not the Platonic ideas. And as I got older and realized that everything and everyone in the world does in time disappear, it came to me that what remains could be taken as a paradigm of all that has already gone. I could now find in one place, an island, a city, a countryside, traces of all the islands, cities, countrysides I have known. I can keep them all available inside myself. As I recall one, I recall and enjoy all. This particular one may now be present, but it is the source for renewed reality, renewed presence, a total vision. In such a way I can appreciate what I have, my family and friends, the day I live, the figure of Christ to which I can still compare myself and everyone else. There is more than enough here to hold in suspense all that once seemed to be doomed to vanish altogether, and without which life would be dismally empty. I might recover what the weight of time had seemed to deprive me of. Augustine's words may not be altogether lost. God, sin, praise, disquietude, may yet regain some status and quietly confront their sad replacements—identity, failure, nostalgia, insecurity— in a historically new and living equilibrium.

WALKING TO MARATHI

When I woke up it was three o'clock. I heard girls laughing. "Gudrun!" "Good night!" And then one of them knocked on a door until she was let in. I got out of bed and stood in the door to the terrace, and saw the white city and the sea sparkling under the moon. There was deep silence now, except for one distant motorbike changing gears on the hill. By four the first rooster would be sending a tentative cry into the darkness of the morning. My vacation had reached its second stage.

Vacations in the Aegean go through three distinct stages for me. The exhaustion after the ordeals of the journey, after weeks of counting the days until we could start. Now the slow-down, forgetting the past, complete disinterest in any future. For the first time in a year I would live in the present alone. Towards the end I would turn instinctively to the future again, seeking ways to justify living.

After going back to bed, I had a complex dream, like others at home, that I could not remember when I woke up, except for the conclusion that all my time was lost or failed or dispersed. It was a summary of the fears of a life that knew no other sureties, at least in the night.

When I was a child I knew that someday I would lose everything I was. Before I became a man I used to wonder what happened to scenes when they vanished. Could there be a restoration? Later I tried to remember steadily as in a painter's landscape the best that I had known. It was an exercise in preserving my identity, a game and a way of forgetting the loss of parents and friends.

Lost time is indelible. No personal fiction ever satisfies me that I can recover it. Not how to live with lost time, but how to live with its pathos. It came to me that Plato may have left us an answer in his world of ideas. Perhaps he was right. Perhaps when all vanishes, this material world which I ache for, could survive in an ideal world that can keep the terrors of night from choking us to death.

Last year we entered an empty bay on the southern tip of Ios, Manganari. On one side there appeared a cluster of white, cubed houses, an uninhabited hotel, a Potemkin village. It was an exhilarating sight, a quintessential Cycladic village in miniature. All winter long back home I was comforted by the memory of its formal purity. Now a year later, looking down on a sleeping town in the moonlight the Platonic image no longer works, and I must deal with dreams more directly.

I say to myself: "I will arise now and walk to Maráthi." How often it seems when a solution falls apart in my hands, I have simply gone for a walk. I have walked from restlessness, and for well-being, but never until now with any hope of exchanging one kind of life for another. At home when I walk along tree-lined roads, I try to sort out thoughts, and sometimes give shape to proclamations, almost as a miniaturist paints a cameo. Walking to Maráthi will not be like that. It is meant to counterpoint, not supplement. I have never been to Maráthi. I have never even heard anybody talk of it. All I know is that it is in the middle of the island, away from beaches, crowds, voices, discos, motorbikes, and buses. It is, as it were, a reserved and secret center of the real life of this part of the world, a safe house.

To get there I will climb the steep hill, repeating in half an hour the two day ordeal of flying across ocean and sailing across sea. I will be so tired that I will be tempted to call it a day. I may not reach Maráthi ever. I do not care what

36

Maráthi is. I only need an excuse to walk away from my bad dreams.

The road to Maráthi was not straight. It meandered between tall walls of stones piled loose. The fields behind them had random shapes. There were no crops, only shaggy goats, sheep huddling under a wall, a fig tree here, a prickly pear there, a scattering of grape vines lying on the parched earth. The houses might have been taken from Manganari and aged before planting, as a Platonic idea goes grey when it is applied to reality. But the pale blue sky was filled with a light reflecting the rocky soil, and the air was soft and dry. Skin, muscles, lungs felt young again. Air, light, wind, silence—"here, buckle!" I can liken it only to what I have been told about the inflowing of contemplation.

When I thought of using Manganari as a Platonic Idea, to save me and my vanished world, I tried to take the picture apart, house from wall from sloping street and waiting for similar parts of islands I had known to match up. And then standing at the top of one street, looking down broad white stone stairs, I would imagine descending. Descending the Platonic stair, I would re-enter the real world of my fears and my past. Here on my safe island I had had to ascend, as in real life, with heart-thumping force, before I could begin to counterpoint discouragement and fatigue.

I reached Maráthi that morning. I was not disappointed. It was no more, no less than I had anticipated. The church had a pink dome like other churches on this island. The school was just a few rows of stone tables and benches in the courtyard of the church. As in dreams there were no people around. And so I saw Maráthi as a dream set-piece, a limit set for an exercise in counterpointing time. Tomorrow I would find another.

By this time I had discovered that however different lost time is from failed time and dispersed time, to counterpoint one is to counterpoint the others. I wonder whether each of us is troubled more by one than by another, more at one time than at another. That is the way it has been for me. I am no longer surprised at the diminished attention to guilt in our day, and the obsession with success and failure, winners and losers. Distinguish as I must between failing in the eyes of others and failing myself. No one finds it easy to be a non-person, to drop out of humanity. When I was young I was convinced I must try to find new words for existential realities. Why now do I have a feeling I have failed? Once I had sat in a classroom listening to Alfred North Whitehead and all the while looking out of the window at the falling leaves in the Yard. I said to myself, "The falling leaves are more real than his 'prehensions'. They are connected with the reality I want to write about someday." And when I read St. Augustine, Kierkegaard and Unamuno, I knew I was reading about my own restlessness and nostalgia. I felt most alive when walking the restlessness out into the country around Oxford and Fribourg. I assumed that if I kept on walking I would never feel I had wasted my time.

I do not think I knew the anxiety of failure until, by the usual reckoning, it was almost too late, when the top no longer spun fast. Until then I felt it was enough to worry about lost time and scattered time. And so walking to Maráthi took on the dimension of a breaking of barriers, one last effort to prove to myself that in reaching a goal I had set I was at the same time living life as it is meant to be lived. I am not sure whether I would have felt I had succeeded if I had not set out again up the hill, this time with my younger son. We set out for Aghia Sophia, beyond Maráthi. We never got there, but went so far that we had to descend a succession of precipitous stony fields to the sea, because we had run out of time. From this I learned that holy wisdom is always out of reach, that one runs out of time no matter what the goal, and above all it is good to have a companion.

In that world of sea and rocks and mountains one can walk nowhere that others have not walked before. My son asked, "Do you think Homer ever came here?" This sea, of a blue so clear and bright. Those other islands in the distance, brown and grey and hazy blue. Those sails, those hulls moving in silence over the water. That line of white at the base of the hills, the harbor we had left hours before. Yes, why not, Homer might have seen all this. He too, above all others, knew what it was like to have left home, to be lost, to have failed. He knew the restlessness, the violence, the disappointments that are part of anyone's life, the terrible need to return to the places where it began, the need to start all over. He knew how life is lived, that one must never give up. He knew one has to try to draw landscapes representing the actual and the ideal, real times and real places and people, set in the stone of similes and metaphors. He had his Fribourg and Charleston in his Troy and Ithaca. So here am I, with my son, high above the Aegean, in Homer's world of islands and cities, wars and dreams. Like Achilles who sat down and wept, like Patroklos, "O rider Patroklos, dying," we too weep for what we have lost, and before dying struggle again for honors and for love of this world one last time. There are only losers in this great frieze, except, as Homer would say, for heroes.

Now as my older son comes in from the cold of Ethiopian malevolence, the dispersal of our family and their coming home remind me that the final problem will always be the scattering of our time, not our failures. Whatever replies we learn to make to the dead and the failed, there is no peace that does not depend on the integrity of privacy, silence and single-mindedness. True peace when it does come is like lying on the sands of Manganari, where even naked bodies become abstract things, where the sun exerts a gentle pressure to hold us in place, and the sand accommodates itself to our special shapes. Reprieve succeeds ordeal and effort; sorting out what one knows and believes precedes the making of a new mindscape. The silences of a day in the sun or on the roads to Maráthi or Aghia Sophia erase the lasting harm of the night sounds between dream and awakening.

I see the little boy from the frozen North waking up in the big room in Charleston in the spring, hearing the fish man calling in the street, the clanging of the trolley bell as it takes the corner. I see the student making his way down the covered stairway from baroque St. Michel to the Gothic cathedral in the lower town. I see the teacher before the fall semester starts sitting on a patch of heath cranberries and watching the subsiding of the sea after a storm. I see the priest holding the hand of a dying friend, shaken by the pleading eyes.

He walked in Charleston and in Fribourg and over the dancing rocks of his island in Maine. He walked in Bujumbura and in Copenhagen and in Monkton. He went through the first part of his life feeling the special tint and fragrance of everything known for the first time. He walked through the middle of life with an abiding nostalgia without object. He seemed to be closing life summarizing what he held dear. He missed the places that he had lived in or visited. He missed them at times even more than he missed the people he had known. Without the places there could be no people. He even missed the places he would never see. He belonged nowhere. There had been no continuing city except in the mind. He was not sure this was what he would have chosen had all options really been his to command. What remained was a respect for character—honesty and vision—and a suspicion that somehow the smell of jasmine in a corner of Athens, of wisteria in a Charleston garden, was trace and sign of the substratum out of which character and mind arise. How lucky he had been not to have had to choose between them. It all came down to a question of what to want, how much, and how, and when. He would still be trying to solve that before the next rising of the moon.

EXERCISES FROM THE LONG RETREAT

I dreamed I had been sent a gilt-edged postcard. On one side there was a picture of Campion Hall in Oxford where I had once lived; on the other, a picture of an imagined convent in middle Europe. A message said: "You are to come here for a retreat." Not long after, I left for a long trip, but to Africa instead of Europe. At Dakar in Senegal I found a garden in my son's house where I could sit quietly and speculate on what my life had come to after all the dreams and all the journeys.

The Jesuit Long Retreat, based on Ignatius Loyola's *Spiritual Exercises*, is intended to last a month. My own Long Retreat had lasted a lifetime already. And after I had retired from work, I began a second Long Retreat within the first, a final strategic withdrawal and summing up. Having done my best to leave behind all distractions, I could concentrate on final victory.

The language of the *Spiritual Exercises* was once well-known. But its terminology is quaint, partly because Ignatius, a Basque, wrote a somewhat uncertain Spanish. This explanation, for example, he would have called an "annotation." A retreat director had to learn to use special words like "principle and foundation," "preludes, points, and colloquies," "election," "examen," "discernment of spirits." Of these, the first prelude, the "composition of place" (a visualization of scenes from the life of Christ) has proved the most distinctive and useful. Each "day" of each "week" was to begin with a meditation on the "mysteries," scenes from the Gospels. The person making the retreat had to pass from image (first prelude) to idea (second prelude), and then consider the idea point by point, concluding with a supplication or colloquy. The whole exercise was intended to help him arrive at a satisfying decision ("election") on how to live his life.

For Jesuits at least, this method of meditation (or contemplation) would become almost second nature, as important for character as the long course of studies was for mind. A religious life that began in the novitiate with a Long Retreat and another Long Retreat in the final year, the Tertianship, continued to be strengthened by annual retreats.

It was not only the structure of the retreat that distinguished the spiritual life of the Jesuit, it was even more its purpose, what Ignatius called its "principle and foundation": to conquer self for the greater glory of God. "Man is created to praise, reverence, and serve God our Lord, and by this means to save his soul."

Ignatius did not say that the world would be saved if all the Jesuits and their followers were, although one may wonder why the world was not saved if so many Jesuits were. In fact, I wonder whether even they were saved, since it does look as if the world has not yet been saved either. If the "principle and foundation" is widely rejected today, it is not, I think, so much because it makes no sense, as because it would seem to exclude so much: nature, the arts, science, human love. Nevertheless, attachment to God and his glory certainly would distinguish someone under this discipline. Whether we can believe in such an attachment at all, it is still quite possible to admire people whose lives are ruled by it.

In Senegal, outside Dakar, at Keur Moussa, there is a Benedictine monastery, founded by monks from St. Pierre of Solesmes Abbey in France. The brothers, half French, half Senegalese, have created a liturgy from Mass and Office that is inspired by both Gregorian and West African melodies. They accompany their singing with 21-stringed Kora, flute, and drums (tam-tam). To be present at Mass in their Rond-champ-styled church—white habits, candles, incense, music—and not be moved one would have to be almost totally encumbered with self. Aesthetic and religious are one. The aesthetic cannot be isolated from the religious, or the religious from the aesthetic. Piety and music serve each other. I found it an exercise that united a story of salvation with exaltations that music by itself is incapable of. What one person is used to as aesthetic (by way of music, poetry, and drama), another recognizes as moral (by way of theology and prayer). The result is one and the same, a transfiguration of the spirit.

It is unfortunate that we have learned to separate feel-ings—aesthetic, erotic, moral, religious—in such a way that it has become almost impossible to think of emotions as direc-tions of the spirit instead of different languages. We have forgotten how to separate those that seize and obsess from those that touch only peripherally: emotions of any kind can do both. There is also the question of where an emotion leads to, and how far. If you begin to suspect that some feelings, some emotional experiences, are pushing you beyond the things you take for granted, you may be surprised to find yourself groping for obsolescent words like "transcend." This is why Ignatius Loyola knew he had to preface his exercises by referring them to a "principle and foundation." St. Anselm's formula for this is "that than which no greater can be thought," the dimension in mind and reality which supplies the "trans-" in "transcend," "transform," and "transfigure."

For Loyola spiritual exercises were strategies for control of self in an intellectual world dominated by the idea and presence of Creator and Redeemer. It was, in our terms, a strategy for personal identity. For him and for us the end of the quest is not to know but to become. Kierkegaard could be a bridge between us: "to find the idea for which I can live and die." Answers must come out of experience, out of a life under discipline. Just as the soldier Ignatius cautioned that the right following of his strategy must be prefaced by finding out where one is ("examen") and a "discernment of spirit," the spirits of consolation and desolation, we too would do well to achieve some understanding of the structure of our consciousness, its dialectic of flight and return, forgetting and discovery.

When I was in Dakar I gave a conference for the faculty of philosophy at the University. I outlined to them the nature of disquietude. Ignatius had suggested that we wait until both consolations and desolations subside before proceeding with the exercises. I, on the contrary, would say that since they can never vanish—because they are parts of the substratum of disquietude, we should attempt to understand their role. We are familiar with the range of disquietude, from boredom and inconstancy (Pascal) to physical and emotional restlessness, social and cosmic insecurity. The shape (as Beckett would say) of Augustine's famous formula defines the role: "You have made us for yourself, and our hearts are restless until they rest in you." We are disquieted so that we may not fancy ourselves better than we are, and so that we might become more than we are. The practical problem is not how to find rest but how to expand longing. Moreover, this is the basic experience not only of saints, like Gregory of Nyssa and John of the Cross, but of great artists.

It is only fatigue that speaks when we sigh, "Oh, I am content at last, I have done all I meant to do." It is not written that in heaven desire must cease, only on earth. The goal accomplished, the insight achieved, is not representative of the whole of recorded experience, only the weak and sorry part. Human glory—for both the seer and the artist—is to believe in the vocation announced by disquietude. At Dakar I wanted to give my conference without notes, and so I took long walks along the Corniche, talking it out to myself. When the afternoon came, I knew what I wanted to say: first, something about the stubborn narrowness of much of contemporary philosophy, and the struggle of a few—Jaspers and Heidegger, for example—to open the horizon again. I tried to say that nothing real should be excluded—that language is but one kind of reality, even if it sometimes appears to be restrictive. I wanted to encourage my listeners to contrast the analysis of language with the classical love of "wisdom." Many find it as difficult to use this word without embarrassment as "transcendence" or "being." I suggested that when you have not forgotten what it feels like to exist, you will not be able to avoid questions that need new philosophical exercises and a different terminology. But because I knew I was addressing philosophers trained to think in Cartesian or structuralist assumptions, I wondered whether I would be understood at all.

I felt I needed to justify myself to myself, as well as to them, and before I knew it, out of my dissatisfaction I began preparing once again as I talked for a conference that I might never give. Not only must we understand what we, and others, experience, we must try to shape experience by our feeling for it, just as artists do. One of the reasons some have returned to Hegel—but not I—is that they sense in his kind of phenomenology not only what he believed to be the dialectical shape of mind and reality, but an ideal for a better world that does not yet exist. Why should something like this not be the end of all vision—to create through the imagination, much as music, dance, painting do, what has never been until we thought it? Why not tell what we have all wanted to hear and see?

46

That was once understood to be the business of philosophy, too; why not again? Plato's world of ideas, Plotinus' nostalgia for the One, Augustine's power of memory, Aquinas' life of contemplation, Kierkegaard's three stages, Jaspers' boundary situations, Heidegger's care, are all amalgams of dream and reality, what we suppose we see and what we hope to see. In a world saddened by the inevitable disappearance of everyone in it, modern consciousness' affair with identity is only to be settled creatively, with self advancing imaginatively beyond self.

It is not enough to be told that the dreams of night are meant to supplement what we know in broad daylight. We are what we dream and know, and also what we feel and imagine. Consider for a moment the Beatitudes from St. Matthew. They appear to be statements of cause and effect. But we need not ask, "Is this a fact?" Instead, "that is how I would have it!" Not promises but prescriptions, and, as with our hearing of music, not analyses but recognitions. We may not have known it before, but that is how we feel.

I have never been tempted to say, "Forget philosophy, it isn't worth it." There is trivial music too, and certainly trivial painting and poetry. Philosophy can be creative, once again. The role of the imagination in human life is the presentation of alternative worlds, internal and external. So there is no reason why we should let ourselves be crippled by scepticisms so thorough-going and exclusive that we deny or reject what is at hand. The source of philosophy, as of the other forms of the imagination, is our absorption in the world and self. Ideas and structures follow. This is the natural order. Be, feel, see, then understand and make.

Plato and Plotinus left us a flawed inheritance in the dualism between becoming and being that has made it almost impossible for anyone today to use the word "being" philosophically. We can no more than Nietzsche believe in an invisible world that is better than the one we are used to. Therefore, we miss the very taste and scent of our ever-present awareness of the reality of self and all that surrounds us. This is the true world, against which we automatically measure the disquietude and frustrations that we spend so much time wrestling with. That is why we need special exercises to restore a strong awareness of the immediacy of things. All the forms of the imagination are such exercises, and probably succeed in this respect more surely than Ignatius' strategies.

When Plotinus wanted to tell us what he meant by the dialectic of self, he used analogies of music and dance. If he had not believed—like Plato and Augustine—that there is an ultimate difference between matter and spirit, body and soul, he might be our most trusted teacher. In the name of the One, he discovered a dialectic a person can live with, and at the same time he lost the very completeness of things that he believed in so passionately. This is why it is so essential today for each of us to think of life as one long retreat, not from becoming, not from body or matter, but from fragmentation of attention that diverts from immediacy and the whole. Exercises of both dream and memory, of longing, of presence and silence, entries into alternative inner space, are equivalents of the spiritual exercises of the Jesuits. Civilized minds need to acknowledge such a parallel and possibility.

The mild sun glanced on the beds of seashells in the garden. Below the patio where parrots screeched, I sat comfortably under a palm tree, sluggish from breathing the wind bearing sand from Mauretania. The Scriabin sonata from the house and the whistle of doves reminded me of home. When I first arrived, I had marked time with desultory reading. But then the diplomats and philosophers departed, and I was free to resume my search for a way from what I knew to what I wanted, from good to better. I had concluded long ago that keeping faith with the past is not enough. My choice, my "election," had always been to build on memory and image, on understanding as well, "such a form as Grecian goldsmiths make," singing to myself and to anyone who would listen "of what is past, or passing, or to come."

THE SLEEPING BEAUTY

I

PROLOGUE

ONCE upon a time most people believed in an order of justice transcending the everyday world. They believed that in spite of appearances all would come right in heaven if not on earth. The time came when this belief became a less active force in men's conscious lives, and yet the belief survived, underground as it were, in literature, where it was called poetic justice. This meant that it was a justice longed for by the poet and his hearers but no longer experienced. But the more implausible this longing became, the less mankind could be persuaded even in literature of an order of justice transcending chance and history. In our time, poetic justice has left serious literature altogether. Its last refuge is the thriller.[1]

Even now the fairy story remains a more trustworthy agent for poetic justice than the thriller—not because it is older or less plausible, but because it is not a product of self-consciousness. You do not have to identify a fairy story with everyday life in order to enjoy it. Everyone likes a fairy story because everyone wants things to come right in the end. And even though to tell a story is to tell some kind of untruth, one often suspects that what seems to be untruth is really a hidden truth. The fairy tales[2] of the Brothers Grimm are full of hidden truths. No one knows the author of any of these tales. Each is authorized by old, primitive longings, promises, and, we can be sure, fulfilments.[3] They represented to those who told them over and over again, a world of presences evoked at the right time in fulfilment of universal needs. That this is really so, is proved by the perennial delight in them of grown-ups as well as of children. But so deep-rooted, so unconscious is this longing in the reader, that he seldom thinks of asking why he responds, even sceptically, to an account of a world he should know is implausible. Yet we need few excuses to think of fairy stories if we need none to read them. If from reading comes a delight, from thinking about them may come some enlightenment,[4] perhaps even a lightening of the burden of everyday life.

Poetic justice is a sentiment, not a fact. The fact, if there is one, is an order of justice. And since we know little of any order of justice beyond the casual justice of courts and human relations, it is the sentiment of justice that we must deal with first. Poetic justice is the literary expression of someone's longing for justice. Some human being has wanted things to come right in the end so badly that he has put justice into a story. And so many others have wanted the same that no one can now identify the author of the tale. The author need not have believed in justice coming to him, but he must at least have been convinced that that is what he needed most. Perhaps he was defiant rather than optimistic. Perhaps longing and conviction came out of disillusionment. He knew the world is not just, but that is how he would have it be if it were possible.

The question for the reader of a fairy story is: "Can I admit that this is how I would have life be, if it were possible?" This is a necessary question because not all expressions of poetic justice do convince one. Take Nahum Tate's altering of the ending of *King Lear*; it is most unconvincing. This is not how things should have ended, with Cordelia alive, these good rewarded and those evil punished. It is not tragic because it is not real, and therefore it is not poetic justice either. For in tragedy there is often a suspicion that the worst is not completely undeserved. Poetic justice convinces only when one can believe in the deserving: good and evil must be easily recognizable. In this a fairy story—unlike *King Lear*—excels. Honesty, courage, effort, beauty, and a good heart, ought not to lose out, and they do not. Justice matches deserving.[5]

Not all fairy stories are equally enchanting. None is more so than the tale of The Sleeping Beauty, or Little Briar Rose.[6] In it a beautiful princess is imprisoned in an enchanted sleep of a hundred years. She is awakened only at the end of this time when a foreign prince passes through the briar hedge surrounding the castle, past the sleeping court, and touches the sleeping princess who awakes at the touch. To those who were contemporaneous with the enchantment, the prince's coming was unexpected, but to those in the know, like the hearers of a tale, the prince had come at the only time, the right time, and in coming fulfilled a promise made long before. In coming he had brought to life the past itself as if no time at all had gone by. Few can read this without feeling the sentiment in the poetic justice, the longing for fulfilment of all that is best in life. We do ourselves injustice if we pretend that this longing is not worth knowing more about.

Grimm's collection of fairy tales is not yet one hundred and fifty years old. It is itself, therefore, a product of modern life, the life beginning after the French Revolution and extending through the nineteenth century to our century of great wars. It was appropriate that, when all old values and beliefs were being discredited by revolution[7] and by the new confident bourgeois civilization, some men should go back, surreptitiously, to the past, for help in surviving in a time when everything spiritual had disappeared but self-confidence. The brothers Grimm were right in sensing that self-confidence is not enough. The rest of the nineteenth century, its individualism in several forms, each bearing its own seed of self-destruction, proved this without the final evidence of a whole world at war. The myth-seekers were looking, beneath and away from the artificial intellectualized civilization of men and books, to the unconscious but no less delighted preoccupation with moral antinomies and moral resolutions. There is no faltering in a fairy story, no question of its values, the deserving or the end.

For the fairy story represents permanent longings and convictions rather than history and change.

So much anyone can see easily. But what one does not usually see is that these longings and convictions relate to a world which is within our grasp, which is actually experienced. We have had the habit of putting this justice in heaven—which, being unseen, is presumed also not real—away from experience. The truth is, we respond delightedly to such a tale as that of The Sleeping Beauty because it is in some way familiar to us. Not only is the longing familiar, the fulfilment is also. This is because we know more of fulfilment than we realize. We know as much about fulfilment as about longing. Contrary to the usual opinion, one can say that the only reason we have and understand longing is that we have and can understand fulfilment.

We cannot long for something we do not know; we know only what is in some way already experienced. However new an experience seems to be, if it fulfils longing it is recognized as familiar as well as new. Fulfilment is in some sense a return. This is illustrated by the tale of The Sleeping Beauty. The princess returns to life; the prince himself comes out of nowhere. And yet to the princess the prince is familiar. To the prince the princess is beyond expectation. There is this paradox in the fairy story that matches the paradox in experience. A fairy story is the story of enchantment. Enchantment is a mixture of the familiar and the unexpected; so is the fulfilment of longing in the story. In experience we know that only something new can fill the emptiness, the frustration, the loss, and yet what we actively look forward to, in longing, is like something we have met somewhere before.

On this face of experience mankind is disposed to deceive itself by looking for obvious large-sized evidence of fulfilment, and also by not really knowing what the signs of fulfilment are. The signs and experience of fulfilment are usually small, insignificant in a world which puts quantity and material advantage before the less visible achievements of character and sensitivity. Perhaps never before has the discrepancy been so great between these two ways of valuing. Perhaps never before has mankind been so demoralized by the suppression of the second.

It is not easy to characterize the twentieth century, not because we are in the middle of it or because we do not know all that can be said of it. The difficulty is that one is depressed by a multiplicity of evidence that all is not going well. Perhaps the most significant fact of the times is the curious intermixture of success and failure. This is a century of homelessness and exile, of nervous disorder and persecution, of actual enslavement and barbaric cruelty. It is also a century of the highest advances in technology and comfort, of the profoundest social and critical sensitiveness. The greater the wisdom and the more widespread the social aspirations, the greater the disillusion with false leaders and false movements. When things go wrong, as they so often do, disillusion then matches expectation. It may not be true that more has gone wrong in this century than in any other; it is certainly true that mankind is more conscious now of its failures, just because it knows so much more surely what it ought to be able to accomplish. For this reason the twentieth century has to be judged in terms of the opposites which make up its power. It is just as false to speak of its homelessness without speaking first of its belief in social and economic justice, as it would be to speak of its technology without speaking of the wars which absorb so much of that technology.[8] And yet it is proper that we should think first of the homelessness that is expressing itself in personal homesickness and longing for lands never seen. If fulfilment must somehow precede longing, it is nevertheless fitting that an understanding of homelessness must precede an understanding of longing and fulfilment.

One should not underestimate our acquaintance with the negative aspects of our time. People do not always wish to be reminded of them, because they have the nineteenth century illusion that if the race is not progressing it ought to be. They resent any implication that life is more complicated than we have been led to think. However much men to-day suppress or ignore depressing estimates of their time, they are all well-acquainted with the facts. What are these facts? There are four, three of which have appeared since the French Revolution. The most notorious of these is the totalitarian reality of slave or police States paralysing human growth and decency.[9] By this reality many millions of human beings have already, within forty years, been killed, mutilated, dispersed, and enslaved. And the rest of the world still lives under the threat of being treated in the same way. Whatever one may say of the causes of this catastrophe—and one of the causes is the legitimate aspiration[10] of the dispossessed to be treated justly, humanly—the channelling of just aspirations into police States, has so far brought only loss and fear to everyone. Against this background human figures even in the politically free countries struggle on, hampered by two more immediate pressures: the continued indifference of the bourgeois mind to individuality[11] and spiritual values on the one hand, and on the other, the accelerating complexity[12] of the demands modern living makes. The fact that most of these demands are trivial does not make them less effective or less noticeable. There is so much to learn, so much to hear about, do, see, so much that changes even while one watches, that life sometimes seems like getting a mailbag full of second-class matter. The effect of these three pressures is simply to make individuals feel anonymous, without a name which can live on in either memory or affection. The person who feels this anonymity in himself, feels himself ceasing to be a person. It may be suggested that one need not be recognized to be a person, that one can get along by oneself.

But this has been proven by the experience of the great isolated figures of the nineteenth century not to be the case. At no other time has mankind given individualism and voluntary isolation so fair a trial. The bourgeois individualism in politics and economics has been no more socially successful than the rebellious isolation of artists and philosophers. Their fruit is their sequel, the present century in which isolation is more widespread, but only because isolation to-day is the enforced isolation of those who are denied individual liberty, the quiet and opportunity to develop their convictions.

The last century knew anonymity too, but it was the anonymity of bourgeois economic individualism which, prophetically, the rebellious artists and philosophers singled out as the flaw of modern life. But the isolated men of the last century did not think of themselves as anonymous. Now no one is in a position to claim that he has escaped anonymity altogether. There is no longer any easy way to avoid the pressures that we have just recounted. The problem is not when will these pressures abate—probably they will not abate, but increase—but how and whether man can be affected by them and still retain his creative powers and social virtues. Isolation was the nineteenth century's answer to anonymity. To-day isolation itself must be regarded as the chief symptom of the pressures on man. To-day isolation and anonymity are synchronous. The resolution of the problem will have to be more positive than isolation, for isolation is now part of the problem. What this resolution is we will not know until we know more surely the problem set in terms of anonymity.

Is anonymity just another word for homelessness? No, it is not. A man who feels anonymous, lonely in a crowd, feels he is missing the distinctness from his neighbour that a name would give him. This distinctness—or distinction, when brought to flower—would matter less if there were not the question of time. With only a few years to maintain or achieve distinctness from other creatures, there is an urgent need to find oneself. But to find oneself is also to find one's place, to belong somewhere, to be part of some space called home.[13] Only at home, only when one is at home with some part of life, does the spectre of anonymity cease to hover. And as long as pressures make anonymous units out of beings who should be persons, these men will feel homeless. The truth is they are rendered anonymous when they are driven from their homes. Anonymity is a special form of homelessness. The worst that can be said of it is that the more anonymously mankind is treated, the less man feels his homelessness. As long as home is remembered, as long as a man is homesick, he still knows what it is to be a person, even if displaced. And so long will he know the simple, if impracticable way back home. That way is the recognition by the home that matches one's own recognition of the place, the family, and the beauty of their presence together. Even without this double recognition, homeless men may at least realize that the key to the passage from anonymity to homelessness is the understanding of non-recognition.

What is it like to be not-recognized?[14] Psychologically speaking, it means that a man is not known as familiar; one has never seen him before. Morally speaking, it means that he is a stranger to others, not familiar. There are occasions when a man is not recognized by someone who has known him. We say that he has been cut and, we might say, cut from a familiar or familial relationship. To be cut is to be betrayed, to have evil done deliberately to one. There is no more embittering experience than this. On the other hand, to be recognized is, at least, to be acknowledged, to have one's presence registered. At best, it means to be taken for what one is. Whichever way one is recognized, the aspect of familiarity is the determinant. Unless a man is taken for or allowed to be familiar in some way, he is not recognized; he is then forgotten. When a man is cut, he is betrayed, and it is as if he were forgotten. No wonder he feels anonymous and homeless. But when he is recognized, he is remembered, and is glad and grateful that someone else has remained loyal to him.

In the twentieth century there are four kinds of pressure which encourage non-recognition, homelessness, and anonymity. We have mentioned three of these already: the reality of collectivist States, bourgeois indifference, the acceleration and overwhelming complexity of modern life. Their effects are seen on both the physical and the psychological levels. Some men are actually herded from their homes to cattle cars; others feel as if they had no homes at all. But the fourth kind of pressure, which we have not mentioned, is the perennial pressure of affliction. Mankind has always suffered, often past endurance. But now suffering is less easily borne than before, for people have every right to expect to be spared suffering by the precautions and therapies of their technology. In addition, most men have no consoling belief in a heavenly justice that will make everything come right, even the most outrageous suffering. Modern values do not encourage stoicism, and modern police techniques make stoicism almost impossible.[15] Thus in the present century men are more prone to the suffering that desolates, that cuts them off from everything familiar, and are less able to bear suffering when it does come.[16]

Only one hundred years ago almost any member of the bourgeoisie could say confidently: "Others are anonymous but not I." And although he might be mistaken, from the point of view of Kierkegaard or Nietzsche, at least we can say for him that there were then many exceptional men, artists, thinkers, writers, scientists, statesmen, of whom no one could have the right to use the epithet anonymous. And yet at that very time the conquest by anonymity was being advanced. By the end of the century Nietzsche was speaking openly of homelessness, for his situation was, as we can now see, a transition from the emphatic self-confidence of exceptionally sensitive men like

Stendhal and Kierkegaard,[17] to the apparent abandonment which obsessed Kafka. Nietzsche was not himself homesick, however clearly he saw the possibility of homesickness for others, for he had no memory of a paradise lost. Homesickness reflects another and better time. The most contrary individualisms of the nineteenth century looked to the future rather than the past. And individualism broke apart just because it wore itself out chasing the future while it lacked a true present. The homesick man, on the other hand, looks to the past not because he does not want the future, but because he wants a true present. The past with which alone he is familiar offers itself to him as a model. Much nonsense has been written about turning the clock back, of burying oneself in days that are well gone, of ignoring what one has or should grasp for the sake of regrets and illusions. However just these fears may often be, they keep one from seeing the utility of homesickness, as a sign in man of his need for a true present.[18]

To be homesick can mean more than to want to go back to the scenes of one's childhood, or even to one's family. "Home is where the heart is,"[19] and one's heart can be almost anywhere. The lines of Burns, "My heart is in the Highlands, my heart is not here,"[20] tell us poignantly of the element of distance[21] between a man and the homeland which is elsewhere. The more anonymous life becomes, the more disquieted a man becomes, the more frequently will homesickness fall upon him, unless he has surrendered to the many demands to depersonalize himself. Homesickness or nostalgia is an involuntary conscience, a moral conscience, positive rather than prohibitory. It reminds a person, by way of giving him the experience, of the good he has known and lost.[22] Nostalgia is neither illusion nor repetition; it is a return to something we have never had. And yet the very force of it is just that in it the lost is recognized, is familiar. Through nostalgia we know not only what we hold most dear, but the quality of experiencing that we deny ourselves habitually. This is why nostalgia is a moral sentiment. It is also the moral sentiment of the present century.[23]

As long as mankind was sure of its ideals and virtues, as long as men knew where they belonged and lived as if they knew, as long as they could believe that there was an order of justice transcending their own mistakes, nostalgia was but one sentiment among many others. But when the ideals and virtues were forgotten or discredited, when the gods died and men themselves were forced into wandering and exile, then nostalgia stood out as a lighthouse to wave the way back to the homeland. Unfortunately, nostalgia is still misconceived by a remnant of shallow optimism, as sickly, illusory, unprogressive. Actually, it is the very opposite, understood by stout souls who, being homesick, are yet not sickly, being realistic, have no illusions, and who, while searching for something abiding, have no use for change for change's sake.

Nostalgia should be valued for the same reason that a fairy story's poetic justice is superior to that of a thriller; it is not deliberately contrived. It is evidence given to persons who need reassurances and direction. Because it is not contrived, we can distinguish it from the more conscious longing that is the open turning away from homelessness to homesickness. Without this evidence one would be justified, as some in our time have believed they were, in waiting for justice to come to them. They have wanted but have not dared to long for fulfilment, and lacking nostalgia have wasted their time. It is not to be doubted that those who wait have been homesick too. We may guess that they too have surrendered to the habit of ignoring the implications of nostalgia. This natural sentiment lives in between waiting and longing, and appears, in the midst of wretchedness and failure, to recall the soul to its inner unity and value. The soul shudderingly draws itself up and offers to the depressed consciousness a psychic experience of presence. In nostalgia one smells and tastes, one responds from the darkest corners of oneself, as a renewed whole, to some reality one loves, a person or a place or even an idea. No longer is there any excuse for waiting; nostalgia is regenerative and requires the starting of life all over again.

This is why it is mistaken to think of homesickness as sickly or unprogressive. On the contrary, it is the soul's natural way of fighting the sickness of despair. And if one understands what is required of one, the effect of nostalgia should be a progress toward presence. But there is no denying that the way of this progress is the way of a return. The way to paradise is at the same time a journey from paradise. This is not as pessimistic as it may sound, for to have come from a paradise is a guarantee of paradise. There are two distinct notions in the phrase "journey from paradise", a phrase suggested to me by Proust's remark that "the only true paradise is the paradise we have lost".[24] The first is the notion that life is a pilgrimage, voyage, or wandering—and the last is certainly the least desirable.[25] The second is the idea of a return. But one can see both ideas in the phrase without being sure what direction the journey is taking. At first glance, one would suppose that he who journeys from paradise is travelling in and towards misery; and surely it would be hard to deny that misery is implied, or that the world does not provide it. A second glance gives one a chance to wonder whether a journey from paradise may not be different from a journey to misery. Can the memory of paradise help to characterize the journey as well as the hardship of the journey itself? If so, is it certain that paradise cannot be regained?

In lingering homesickness just as in short intense nostalgic flashes, paradise is, as it were, regained. One feels as if one were there, except—and this is the other side of nostalgia—one knows one is not there. The gain and the loss are inextricably mixed, and the effect on the soul is to remind one that one misses and has missed chances to be and see as one should.

Without nostalgia a man would have no way of telling himself what life ought to be like, for no purely rational plan or decision can include the principal character of happiness and fulfilment, namely, presence. Nostalgia makes presence, theatrically, but convincingly, for it represents the thing or person or place we care for as an oasis of presence in a desert of loss. It is this juxtaposition of the negative with the positive, this enveloping of the negative, of change, of disappearance, of our having lost touch, of our having diminished, which seems to isolate the good for us and momentarily stop time. If you say that nostalgia is not the only means of achieving presence, we should have to admit that love does this also. But love and possibly certain artistic and contemplative experiences are defined by their sense of a presence which wells up through the surrounding, shifting, arbitrariness of consciousness and environment. We are not talking of essences, with which a man cannot be totally identified, but with presences which seem to meet him half-way. There is no question here of distance, of objectivity. That has its place, but not where justice and paradise are concerned. Anonymity, homelessness, waiting and longing are not to be satisfied except by counter-currents which sweep them along. To journey from paradise, in this sense, means to journey towards the end that was the beginning. This is a return, therefore, to what has been known and loved. If one objects to this, one must first prove that there is nothing worth having known and loved, and then that it is impossible to be made happy by returning to them. Perhaps such a sceptic should also wonder whether his diagnosis of human restlessness is thorough enough to let him be satisfied with restlessness itself as the only mode of existence. For there is no alternative. The choice is between yielding completely to time and change or trying in some way to find that principle of identity and integrity and satisfaction which the restlessness itself tells us we need but do not have.[26] Platonists and Christians alike have

23

assumed in this manner that man is meant to have unity, integrity, peace, and a true present.[27] But none has realized that the model and the instinct is nostalgia, the sentiment of presence, which phoenix-like springs from the ashes of disquietude, sentiment of emptiness and alienation.

At this point, if not before, some people cannot help asking, out of their restlessness, whether nostalgia can possibly be thought of as a way of life. Should one, to be blunt, be nostalgic? The answer is, one is already nostalgic if one is sensitive to one's failure to achieve the presence that signifies the reality of justice and happiness. The problem is to understand the nostalgia, not make it. And there is no doubt that true understanding is itself a way to happiness. For how can one search for presence if one does not know what to search for? And how can one know what presence is, what it feels like to be near it, unless one has been near it and has reflected enough on it to know it? The search and then the practice of presence are further steps and stories, but the understanding of the direction and the end is the necessary beginning of the ascetic journey. Asceticism need not and should not imply starvation or self-laceration; it is simply the concentration, the recollection, of all the energies of body as well as spirit, on some high task. The task nostalgia sets man again and again is the need and beauty of presence.

Presence is not a familiar philosophical term, for it is only since the first world war that it has been deliberately used by some European philosophers.[28] This is an interesting fact, because presence is the new ontological expression spontaneously put to use in response to the longing arising out of homelessness. It has always had several different but allied usages. Before all others it has meant "being".[29] It is, in fact, the concrete way of denoting being or existence. But it cannot be adequately explained only as the equivalent of being and/or existence. It suggests that some being is actively, almost vibratingly related to one. And it is not much of a jump from here to the psychic presences that are known as ghosts. A presence is a being which is intimate with us.[30] Wordsworth's "presence that disturbs me" says much the same thing. But whether physical or spiritual, palpable or purely psychic, a presence is something which moves one. Perhaps we should remark that of a presence it is impossible to say whether the moving is exclusively physical or spiritual, the two are so confused.

If the presence is friendly, something in us is moved in return, and we are fulfilled. Justice is done. The sleeping beauty awakes. If the presence disturbs as a source of hurt or panic, one may have to ask whether justice has not been done here too. Who knows just what one deserves? Who knows also when the final decision on one's case has been handed down? But however sceptical, however we hold ourselves in suspense or are held down by circumstances, we do meet presences if we have not inured ourselves to their influence. And whether or not we are educated to appreciate their importance, we feel instinctively at the time that we are experiencing something special. Of all these experiences, that of love, with its mixture of giving and wanting, is the prototype. The more anonymous and homeless men become, the less they experience love in its fullness. As love recedes, only nostalgia remains to recall them before they accept their abandonment. Such an acceptance makes men into barbarians and slaves. An understanding of homesickness is their last chance to return to the world of presence before they are lost forever in a world ruled by hate and alienation.

There is no word for "being" that has so many implications as "presence": metaphysical, moral, psychological, religious. And we expect this of a word which, in English at least, has several undertones. "The present" is temporal.[31] The present is what we never fully attain except in recollection, memory and reflection, and in longing. "A present" is a gift from elsewhere to us. A present is what a person needs who knows he is not self-sufficient, and who can respect the presence of another. "The presence" of another is the available intimacy[32] which promises to give what we need for fulfilment.[33] Wherever there is this awareness of intimacy, of the chance that one may be given what one longs for and needs, one can be sure there is a "real presence". There are unreal presences, evil, empty, deceiving. There are also the substantial presences which admit us to their intimacy in the fullness of time. It is appropriate that the Christian religion, a religion depending so much on an encounter of eternity with history, should speak of the sacramental incarnation as a real presence which the faithful approach in prayer and expectation. Prayer is the religious equivalent of longing. Whenever longing approaches fulfilment, it is approaching a real presence, in loving as in praying.

These four undertones of presence correspond to the four implications, the metaphysical, the moral, the psychological, the religious. They define the shape of the world that nostalgia dreams of. In this world where anonymity and noise and change reign, where every day homelessness is confirmed rather than diminished, it has, paradoxically, become possible to see more clearly than ever before the life that mankind probably enjoys less than at any other time. Never before has the world wanted presence enough to make clear what it is. Can we practise it once we too know it again? That is the problem for further searching and exercising. But there is no need for searching until we begin to recognize the presence that is lost to us in our homelessness and anonymity.[34] The tale of The Sleeping Beauty is a tale of just such a recognition.

II

THE TALE

1—MORNING AND AFTERNOON

"A long time ago there were a King and Queen who said every day,
        Ah, if only we had a child!
but they never had one.
  But it happened that once when the Queen was bathing,
a frog crept out of the water on to the land,
and said to her,
        Your wish shall be fulfilled;
          before a year has gone by,
        you shall have a daughter.
What the frog had said came true,
and the Queen had a little girl who was so pretty
   that the King could not contain himself for joy,
   and ordered a great feast.
He invited not only his kindred, friends, and acquaintances,
but also the Wise Women,
  in order that they might be kind and well-disposed towards the
There were thirteen of them in his kingdom,   [child.
  but, as he had only twelve golden plates for them to eat out of,
one of them had to be left at home.
The feast was held with all manner of splendour,
  and when it came to an end,
the Wise Women bestowed their magic gifts upon the baby.
One gave virtue, another beauty, a third riches,
and so on with everything in the world that one can wish for.
  When eleven of them had made their promises,
suddenly the thirteenth came in.
She wished to avenge herself for not having been invited;
  and without greeting or even looking at anyone,
she cried with a loud voice,
        The King's daughter shall, in her fifteenth year,
         prick herself with a spindle, and fall down dead.
  And without saying a word more,
she turned round and left the room,
They were all shocked,
but the twelfth, whose good wish still remained unspoken, came
                [forward.

27

And as she could not undo the evil sentence, but only soften it,
she said,

> It shall not be death,
> > but a deep sleep of a hundred years,
> > > into which the princess shall fall.

The King, who would fain keep his dear child from the misfortune,
gave orders that every spindle in the whole kingdom should be burnt.
Meanwhile, the gifts of the Wise Women
were plenteously fulfilled in the young girl,
> for she was so beautiful, modest, good-natured, and wise,
> > that everyone who saw her was bound to love her.

It happened on the very day when she was fifteen years old,
the King and Queen were not at home,
and the maiden was left in the palace quite alone.
So she went round into all sorts of places,
looked into rooms and bed-chambers just as she liked,
and at last came to an old tower.
She climbed up the narrow winding staircase,
and reached a little door.
A rusty key was in the lock,
and when she turned it, the door sprang open,
and there in a little room sat an old woman with a spindle,
> busily spinning her flax.

> > Good day, old mother,

said the King's daughter,
> > What are you doing there?
> > I am spinning,

said the old woman,
and nodded her head.
> > What sort of thing is that,
> > > that rattles round so merrily?

said the girl,
and she took the spindle,
and wanted to spin, too.
But scarcely had she touched the spindle
> when the magic decree was fulfilled,
> and she pricked her finger with it.

And in the very moment when she felt the sting,
she fell down upon the bed that stood there,
and lay in a deep sleep.
And this sleep extended over the whole palace.
The King and Queen,
> who had just come home,
> and had entered the great hall,
> began to go to sleep,
and the whole of the court with them.
The horses, too, went to sleep in the stable,

the dogs in the yard,
the pigeons upon the roof,
the flies on the wall,
even the fire that was flaming on the hearth became quiet and slept,
the roast meat left off sizzling,
and the cook who was just going to pull the hair of the scullery boy
[because he had forgotten something,
  let him go and went to sleep.
And the wind fell,
and on the trees before the castle, not a leaf moved again.''[35]

EVERY fairy tale has several acts, corresponding to the chronology of the experiences through which the figures—and the hearers—pass. The first act differs only superficially from one tale to another, for in many tales the events and personages are similar. In hearing the first part of The Sleeping Beauty, and in following its account of prophecy, promise and gift, discontent, threat and bewitchment, we follow the themes which characterize the foreground, not only of this and other fairy tales but of much of life as well. The opening of this myth reveals the tensions and conflicts, the fears and the desires of human nature and history. We shall not know whether there is more to the world than promise and defeat until we have a clearer view of the relation of promise to defeat.

There is no more suitable approach to this story than by way of the metaphysical analysis of Gabriel Marcel. His thinking is doubly relevant because he has outlined and interpreted the polarities we so commonly meet in person and in society, and because he has introduced a new philosophical category, *presence*, which is lacking in life and to be found in story. If we can understand *presence*, we shall understand the search for the order of poetic justice which is the order of folklore. It is not necessary for Marcel himself to make every one of these connections for us. It would be more honest to say that through his understanding of *presence*, we are introduced to an entirely new approach to that permanence that haunts both philosophers and poets. Marcel's categories bespeak the moral world as everyone experiences it, and without distortion. He belongs to that very small series of European philosophers who have seen certain things so clearly that they have been able to illuminate their insights like the capitals in school primers.

Marcel is a concrete philosopher; and his philosophy of presence is an ethic of existence. Much has been written since the war about existentialism; much confusion and obtuseness have accompanied this most recent philosophy. But it has become clear that to be an existentialist is first of all to believe that the occupation most worthy of a man is to reach for what is real via inwardness. This involves a transformation of the order in which the human mind has been working, from the arbitrary and abstract to the concentrated and concrete. It is an encouragement to proceed from concrete to concrete, subordinating all one's faculties in this pursuit of the real. This reversal in thinking would be called, in a more religious age, contemplative. Formerly one could say that metaphysics and anthropology had no connection; now they seem inseparable. The fact is not that man no longer wants to know Being; on the contrary, he wants so much to know what is real, after centuries of neglect, that he is exploring the profound tendencies in his own nature that promise to lead him there. It is no absurd coincidence that in the hundred years that man has become most acutely aware of his isolation from himself, his fellows, nature, and God, he should at the same time begin to look within himself for both causes and resources. This is the "ontological hunger" which characterizes times of danger; for Plato the dying of a city, for Augustine the dying of an empire, for us the dying of a God. And in no other philosopher to-day can one find the human condition and contemporary society so dispassionately and yet so expertly dissected, as in Gabriel Marcel's writings. Without the polemic of Kierkegaard, or the obscurity of Heidegger, the nausea of Sartre, Marcel has brought out in his plays, diaries, and critical essays the same clear-eyed moral world of the foreground of the tale of The Sleeping Beauty. But with a difference —you start reading the fairy tale, knowing that there will be an enchantment, knowing that you too will be enchanted. After reading Gabriel Marcel you realize that the enchantment is in the drama, not in the analysis. By analysis one is enlightened rather than charmed. Marcel is first and foremost a philosophical moralist; his dramas exist for the sake of his philosophical works, they provide the very best illustrations of his themes.

Marcel prefers to speak of "concrete philosophy" rather than existential philosophy, "a concrete metaphysics in tune with the deepest notes of our personal experiences". In English "concrete" does not necessarily suggest "personal" but rather utilitarian, practical. This is one of the many instances in which one sees that English lacks transparent terms for the individual's concern with his nature as both human and person. "Personal" itself too readily suggests that which has nothing to do with anybody else, like underwear or correspondence. Either such words are commonly vulgarized or, equally unfortunate, they sound flat and abstract. Part of the difficulty English speakers have in reading European philosophers comes from their feeling that much is being made of little, that quite ordinary, even trivial experiences are being overcharged to the point of nonsense or sentimentality. However complex the reasons for this are, and they are related to a long indifference to much that Europeans have found central to life, we ought to be on guard against a disposition to see in a three-dimensional word only a two-dimensional experience. This is easier for those who, like Marcel himself, take it that "existence is not separable from a certain astonishment", and for those who are indifferent to academic philosophy. Marcel's philosophy is much closer to poetic and religious experience than to the problems that professional philosophers in England and America have set themselves. Whoever is attentive to personal experiences should be able to understand Marcel when he says: "I can be creative as a philosopher only for so long as my experience still contains unexplored and uncharted zones." His "passionate longing for the unknown", for "a universality not of the conceptual order", his opposition to philosophers who "ignore the personal, ignore the tragic, ignore the transcendent", and who "end by ignoring presence", set him apart from the man who has a corner of life taped off by categories and routines that he no longer questions. This is the most durable habit of the bourgeois mind—already almost two centuries old—and its only passion, the disposition to conserve its ego by denying what it cannot understand or feel. Marcel, with a wider conflict in mind, himself makes much of this disposition to *refuse*, and he opposes this refusal by *invoking* reality.

In his plays he deals with reality as subjects, while as a philosopher he writes on the opacity of the mind to transcend objectivity. "It is in drama and through drama that metaphysical thought grasps and defines itself *in concreto*." Even his philosophical writings are in manner dramatic, in the form of diaries, lectures, and reviews. He has written no formal treatise —not even his Gifford Lectures are that—his writings are musings rather than geometrically developed arguments. He may begin from the scene closest to him: "I wrote to A." "I talked to C." "I promised N." "I realized for the first time when I crossed the Montagne Sainte-Geneviève." "About N.'s suicide." "While we were walking yesterday on the hills above Mentone." This is not the way of the professional philosopher to-day—and Marcel knows it. But it was the way of Plato, Augustine, Pascal, Kierkegaard, Nietzsche, Unamuno. The idea begins to come at a certain place, near a certain lake, beside a certain rock, and forever after it is associated with its place. Man is in places, as surely as he is at all; and it is the concrete philosopher whose temper does not let his reader forget this. Man is not mind.

But after saying so much one admits that Marcel's dramaturgy is discursive rather than emotive. His explanations never depart from the level of unimpassioned discourse, and while he speaks often of "mystery" and "inexhaustibility" he himself seems to leave no corners unlighted. His writings do not have the quivering half-lights of sunrise from a sleeping-car that one gets in Proust, for example. They are, however, marked, as Proust's, by an apparently inexhaustible scrupulosity. And even if the end of a probing seems inconclusive, it is only because the dramatist has put off the rest for another day. His disquisitions are here and there analytically exhausting in the manner of a moral theologian, a product of a highly refined conscience. He has promised a dying friend that he will revisit him. At the moment he promised he had been filled with compassion. Later the compassion fades and the promise feels less binding. But is it? And then, over the body of his friend he writes, so expertly, of the causes and consequences of betrayal. In the end the promise is fulfilled with true compassion. His writings encourage and enlighten rather than move. And that is a great deal, for we should not forget that what he enlightens us about are not ideas but experiences.

We should not forget either that like Jaspers or Buber, with whom he has affinities, he always thinks in terms of the persons of a dialogue. Jaspers's emphasis on communication, on the irreducible antinomies within experiences; Buber's quest for that which is "between" the "I and the Thou"; all find their counterparts in Marcel's dramatic confronting of his philosophical categories with each other as with *dramatis personae*. As if in commentary on Conrad's plots, his thinking keeps moving in a series of simple antinomies: mystery and problem, fidelity and betrayal, absence and presence. One might get the impression that this is a philsophy of patches. Actually, the contraries fit like Chinese boxes. Life is compounded of what one can measure, deal with—what Marcel calls problems, functions, techniques, what we might call jobs, position, comfort, security, success, and what one cannot measure or deal with—what he calls mystery, what we might call adventure, flirtation, surprise, exploration. The land of the measurable is that Apollonian world of light, health, and prophecy that Nietzsche wrote of in *The Birth of Tragedy*. The land of the immeasurable is the land of "presence". The former is the world of history, as those historians Tolstoy quarrelled with in *War and Peace* thought of history. The latter is the world of drama, of persons, where the only measure comes from the dramatic form itself, but which threatens to break through the dramatist's control, imposing on the privacy of the audience.

Marcel, like Pascal of whom he may be said to be the only true inheritor, thinks in terms of either-or's. But these are not the conventionally distinct sheep and goat antinomies where one either has no real choice or where the choice seems so obvious as to make the choice too easy. It is not possible to choose either one or the other of the sides of Marcel's antinomies. Both are real and in some way necessary. But there are people who would attempt to ignore one side altogether, and it is against this exclusion that Marcel has always fought. If we can say, for example, that his distinction between problem and mystery is the prototype of all the rest, we must then say that life does have problems as well as mysteries. It would be foolish to try to deny this, but not nearly so dangerous for humanity and history as to deny—and certain pressures would have us—the mystery in persons and other reality.

At different times Marcel seems to have stressed one antinomy rather than another. He has in fact moved from the epistemological to the metaphysical, by way of the ethical. But it is the ethical which he worked consistently at in the thirties, which has come to dominate his philosophical writings and his plays. In the thirties he wrote much about fidelity and betrayal. Why then? Is it not obvious that to an observer of integrity—and

34

there were many then—the thirties were a decade in which the carefreeness of the twenties was finally nurturing rotten fruit: the depression, broken international pacts, broken private lives, civil wars, the great war itself? It was a time when an eager social and political conscience succeeded the fashion for experiment of the twenties. What was lacking, as Marcel simply saw it, was a "fidelity considered as a recognition of something permanent". Ever since the first world war ended men had taught themselves to acknowledge promises only when it was convenient; they had come to identify their lives with whatever they were doing at the moment. Having tried to get the most out of a life held up for four terrible years, they had developed the habit of submerging their natural sense of permanence and loyalty. The depression marked the end for many people of their experiments in relativism. And while for most men the thirties were the decade when success began to mean less than security for the first time, for others it was a time of temporary renewal of faith in ideas, causes, parties, even friends. For many young men and women especially, it was a decade of nervous, last-minute faith in social justice, born too late to prevent the final upheaval of the nations.

Marcel's basic ethical antinomy of fidelity and betrayal can now be understood in terms of a " phenomenology of being and having" which reflected the moral change of interest from possessiveness to reality, from the twenties to the thirties. And it has since become habitual for Marcel to retain this moral cast even when he is speaking of metaphysics or epistemology. Since the second war he has not made as much of fidelity, possibly because he found in "mystery" and "presence" more positive expression of the direction in which his thinking on fidelity had always been taking him, or perhaps because the war and the occupation encouraged exploration of the metaphysical basis of an ethics so wantonly betrayed.

From the start, fidelity, and later presence, had three aspects:

the ethical notion of disposability, the metaphysical notion of permanence, and the epistemological notion of mystery. Marcel was not thinking of fidelity as consistency, for that can be foolish or cruel, but as the attitude of a being disposed to recognize another person in the fullness of his separateness. This cannot happen unless one recognizes oneself as in some way separable from all the extraneous possessions and attainments that make personal relations so tenuous. Fidelity always has this double recognition, of self as well as of others. And the permanent interest of the self should never be confused with those possessions and attainments which can be taken away as easily as they were acquired. What one is, is not what one has. Nor should one be to others according to their rank or one's own success. Others should be interesting to us in proportion to their having an existence separable from their achievements. This may seem a commonplace of moralism; it is Marcel's distinction that he not only continues to analyse the world in terms of it but shows what is involved in fidelity, in being rather than having.

For many men a failure to attach oneself to certain positions or possessions "countenances despair", only because of an initial assumption that to be is to have. Marcel not only maintains that to be is not the same as to have, he warns against hoping that one can be without having. He speaks of the "relative dependence of being and having". We have, in the first place, to have bodies in order to be at all. And, as is obvious, we must have much more to exist and be comfortable. But "we show what we have; we reveal what we are." What have we that cannot be shown? Are we someone who can only be revealed? Have we any idea of the difference between showing and revealing? Marcel thinks not. And, we may add, neither does Ortega.

We are at the mercy of techniques, of machines, gadgets, advertising, and while submitting pleasurably to them we know very well they are treacherous and evanescent. The pleasure we get from the very things we are intelligent enough to distrust is that they distract us from the arduous, subtle quest for some permanence in life. Having gone through two great wars, a depression, and many neuroses, we are well fitted to half-believe that we are made by circumstances rather than by our own searching. The world really does look problematical, circumstantial, external to our wishes, political rather than personal. It really does look like a world which can be measured and studied and manipulated; but it is a world also which is indifferent to the individual. Problems are there to be licked. When a man suddenly discovers, as some do, that some problems cannot be licked, he breaks down. No other age has had so many crocks as ours; and yet our time has not set before it goals any more difficult to attain, given the superior technical and critical means. No wonder Marcel has come to speak of this as a "broken world". "Men have looked for unity outside themselves instead of where it is, within."

In the second stage in Marcel's development he has sought to clarify his view of that other world, the metaproblematic, or world of presence. He never treats it apart from the world of the problematic because he knows that ontological distinctions cannot be separated from the problem of despair. He says, paradoxically, that "our condition requires a kind of systematic sealing off of mystery" (or presence, or being). We are made limited, embodied; and our essence is as restricted as our physique. Our powers are not without limit; we can be only so long and do only so much. You can "consider Being as the principle of inexhaustibility"; you cannot consider your own life as inexhaustible. And yet it is when you treat life as a series of positions which we can approximate and exhaust that life seems empty, futile. There is some instinct in men, some "suppressed dynamic", for that which is inexhaustible, whether it be love or knowledge. We could welcome the chance to get beyond that precious autonomy which no solving of problems ever completely satisfies. To be without freedom is not to be a man; but to have one's freedom continually unsatisfied is to miss a proper field for one's energies.

This is not to say that Marcel is looking for an unknowable God. The mysterious is not, for him, the unknowable. It is within the realm of the intuitively known—or what Pascal calls the "esprit de finesse" or order of charity. Mystery is essentially shareable. Now this is not what we are accustomed to think about a "mystery" which we commonly associate with some gap in knowledge, something that has not been solved yet. For Marcel mystery is that which is inexhaustible yet somehow comprehensible. Presence and mystery are the same thing. We can understand this best if we turn to the ethical meaning which presence has. Marcel uses the example of a man who is in the room with me but who only knows me in my capacity of teacher or customer, for whom I, as I know myself, simply am not present. His relation to me is no different from his relation to a cat or a telephone, to any object of his interest or business. He is not with me, but at me. Who I am he does not need to know. I am his statistics. If he does not have me "taped" and feels he ought to have, he may be angry or upset. Few people can face the quiet presence of inexhaustibility; few authors nowadays have the imperturbability and high purpose that Thomas Mann impresses on us in his dictum: "Only the exhaustive can be truly interesting." (Is that why he never seems to have finished?) As a result, few people, save for the sake of formal consistency, present themselves to others or expect others to be present to them. For Marcel a man "is not a being unless he is a presence"; otherwise he is merely an object of one's attention, a case.

How does a man appear present? Marcel speaks of presence "as a kind of influx". But one need not do anything. "There is a way of listening which is a way of giving." "Presence is something which reveals itself immediately and unmistakably in a look, a smile, an intonation, or a handshake." A man who is present to another can be counted on. Circumstances will not alter his promise or his readiness. To be present is to see someone as a "you" rather than an "it". To be present is to be faithful, not to an abstract principle but to the particular need and character of the person before one. "To be incapable of presence is to be in some measure not only occupied but encumbered with one's own self." The more pre-occupied with self and the problems and achievements of the self the less interesting the person is apart from his achievements and ambition, and the less capable of finding anyone else interesting unless as a case. "The self is always a thickening."

There are two attitudes one can assume towards another person: that of spectator—looking *at* him, or that of witness—being *with* him. The former sizes up the object of his attention; the latter simply attends. The closeness implied in attending characterizes one's sense of presence. Whatever or whoever is present, is a presence, has invaded my being somehow. This invasion is precisely what we fear, because we have identified our privacy with our possessions and fear robbery. But we cannot be robbed of character; there is something in us that can successfully resist possession most of the time. Whatever it is, it is not any complex of fears and desires, or the ambitions the senile individualist associates with being autonomous. It is the autonomous-minded man who makes the best spectator; he has no sympathies, no pity, no love to interfere with his intention to abstract problem from person. But "as soon as we are in Being, we are beyond autonomy . . . the more I am, the more I assert Being, the less I think myself autonomous." The more I assert that someone else is, the more I witness to his special reality as he reveals himself to me, the more I rise above the limits of time, space, and condition. The non-disposable man has no hope. He is at the mercy of time and situation. He is anxious. He has no joy. "The capacity to hope diminishes in proportion as the soul becomes increasingly chained to its experiences." It increases the more one witnesses the revelations of other selves.

When in the presence of another person, one owes it to the other to be for a while passive, so that the full measure of the other can be disclosed. This is not the way we usually behave. We have something to do with someone else, something to see him about, something to tell or find out. We see no point in waiting. Perhaps there is none in most encounters. And yet Marcel has been trying to show that if one does not make full provision for the recognition of others—and the king in the tale of The Sleeping Beauty had not—then willy-nilly one enters a world of discontent and consequent betrayal. The only alternative is to practise the Christian virtues of "patience and humility, virtues whose very names to-day are forgotten". Patience and humility have become euphemisms for resignation and usually do not remind us of an attentiveness to that which transcends change, whether in nature or personality.

One can understand now why Marcel objects to Sartre's nausea and Sartre's inability to believe that love can be unselfish, why he admires, on the contrary, both Rilke and Peter Wust who have, as he says, "a piety towards souls and things of which I think we have to-day to rediscover the secret". He says that Rilke avoids the danger even Christians touched by grace fall into: he never despises things. Rilke never rejects creatures as evil. And yet he does not want everything "unveiled", or as Rilke himself said: "I am totally denuded of curiosity about life, my own future, the gods." How far this statement is from the problematic world where curiosity and energy reign, where the individual feels a failure unless he is "on the go", "in the swim", "in the know"! The opposite, however, is not passivity or resignation, quietism or fatalism; as Marcel sees it, "the domain of the metaproblematical coincides with that of love". Perhaps "piety" is more persuasive because more unusual. By this he is thinking of a watchful receptivity which is another name for creativity. And he says that Rilke rather than Nietzsche or Kierkegaard had this and understood it. This contemplative virtue called piety is far from the modes of interest of Nietzsche and Sartre. If piety stands for creativity in the sphere of artistic production, it stands also for devotion in man's relations with persons, whether human or divine. In another dimension still which Marcel refers to in his remarks on Wust, man can contrast his own unquiet nature with restful, inevitable Nature. Of course, man's relations to nature are determined by his own attitudes; nature is certainly not always restful. We know the September sea; others know dust storms. But we can understand this piety if we recall that climate of familiarity and naturalness which we associate with Tolstoy's two great novels. In both there is an active, living receptivity which is both loving and enduring. In his essay on Wust, Marcel says that we can regain the lost paradise of instinctive piety (of childhood)—so similar in result to Tolstoy's—because we have a principle other than self within us. And we can have piety even towards ourselves because "we are not our own masterpieces". "What is deepest in me is not of me." This is a more positive way of saying, as Proust does: "We are not at our own disposal." However little this may have meant to Proust, is it not clear that, like his famous elegy on the death of Bergotte, it is a far cry from his usual belief that "man is the creature that cannot emerge from himself"? It is "the cracks in Proust's universe", as Marcel calls them, and the enchantment of his art, his own piety towards the reality of the past, "the eternal truths", "the idea of existence", that to some extent assuage Proust's bitterness when he says: "The only true paradise is the lost paradise." To say that man is not at his own disposal need not mean that "what is deepest in me is not of me". But Marcel is willing to start from even that admission. "Proust was right; we are

not at our own disposal. There is a part of our being to which
strange, perhaps not altogether conceivable conditions give
us sudden access; the key is in our hands for a second, and a
few minutes later the door is shut again and the key disappears.
I must accept this fact with shame and sorrow."

Marcel understands and values piety, in Rilke and Wust;
he values silence in Max Picard, but he himself excels in more
active virtues. He is, even as dramatist, a discursive philosopher
rather than a contemplative. Whether through characters in
plays or through notes in his diaries, he explores his categories
with tenderness and patience and minuteness. As we have
seen, his categories always express some fundamental polarity,
and the polarity can always be reduced to experiences and
sentiments through which man either transcends (for Nietzsche,
"surpasses") himself or does not. As Marcel says, in his essay
on Rilke: "Let us remember that there is a side of the world
which is not turned towards us." The soul is a voyager ("Homo
Viator"). Man is an itinerant, and if a stable order is to be
established in the broken world, it will be by men aware of
their wandering. The human voyage takes place in a human
sea, but its home port which is also its destination, is elsewhere.

The character that Marcel gives Rilke, "a witness to the
spiritual", we must give Marcel. It is his bearing witness in
so many ways of an elsewhere that should be a here, of "a
metaphysics of 'at home' ", that makes it easy for us to see
at last that his ethical categories of love, fidelity, and hope are
the theological virtues of faith, hope, and love. We live in a
world where treason is made easy, where hardness of heart
alternates with despair; we have within us, and in certain
witnesses around us, glimpses into a world of loyalty, warmth,
and hope. The key to the door, which is so often shut, to that
better world, is held by the man or woman who preserves in
active form humility and piety. There is little gentleness left
in this world, and what little there is, is sometimes preserved

just by lacking the vision which can take in the world to its depths. "At every level of being, self-destruction is taking place," as men struggle to preserve sanity and liberty. Only in the piety which both fondles natural things and at the same time looks beyond nature for that principle of fullness which nature and humanity attest to, only in man's quest for fullness will the human emptiness and drabness be transfigured.

It is interesting that Marcel should speak of fullness-emptiness as more important to man than one-many. Maybe it is merely truer to the situation of our century that we should need to be filled rather than need to be one, or truer still that we need to be filled so that we may be one. Maybe that is the way it always has been, and it is the progress of our time that we see it. No matter—what does matter is that it is by means of fullness that we can detect the real estuary in Marcel between his exploration of our nature and the theological virtues which so far are parallel in name only. One does not need to mention God to make something of Marcel's distinctions. He has not meant to write a *Summa Contra Gentiles* for our time. He has not set out to prove God's existence, nor has he used the categories of religious experience for the sake of a life which is only a "being-unto-death". All his categories are obviously borrowed from religious experience; and if they do make some sense, it is because man can catch the faint melody of divine things within experience which these categories sing. And Marcel knows this and is satisfied.

Let a man be haunted by memories of living fuller than his own, let him be haunted by a longing for fulfilment, for what has not yet been said or sung or seen or done or made—that man knows the sentiment of fullness. Fullness is not "problematical"—a word meaning contingent as well as solvable; it is, quite appositely, both sure and inexhaustible. It is, therefore, not at our fingertips, not under control, at our command. It is not ours to dispose of. If we know what this fullness is, without having experienced it more concretely than in nostalgia, longing, haunting, encounters, is it not because we have been *given* a taste of it? Is fullness not ours by gift, and that is why not ours to dispose of? And we do not give even this knowledge to ourselves, but like the charity spoken of in the New Testament, it comes down from on high, or up from the past. "Charity thought of as presence, as absolute disposability", is the influx of the sentiment of fullness which gives Marcel the right as a Christian philosopher to make use of the terms of religious experience without sanctifying them with genuflections. "At the heart of charity is presence in the sense of the absolute gift of one's self." To be present is to be ready to dispose of oneself, to give oneself, to make a present of oneself, to fill the emptiness that aches.

The initial act of giving, of presence, is that "ontological mystery" of Christ's sacrifice and the daily sacrifice of the Mass, "the real presence". "The Church is a perpetual witness" to this first gift. God is "absolute presence", and "can only be given to me as absolute presence in worship". This gift is the inflowing of grace, the manifestation of which is often confused with charm. Charm simply tells of abundance and assurance, no matter what their origin; grace should testify to an inner light which has been lent by another order altogether. Just as in Holy Communion one gets in touch with grace through "the real presence", so in human intercourse, when touched by other lives we fortify ourselves (com-mune) through each other's attentiveness. Emil Brunner, thinking along similar lines, identifies communion with presence, a communion in which the individual is present for the God who is present for him. In this experience of mutual giving, man becomes purified in reality, as the spectator of a tragic drama is psychologically purified by the theatrical sacrifice. In both experiences, in the real and in the theatrical sacrifice, the individual is filled; far from being a mere emptying of pity and fear or heartache and boredom, catharsis and communion fill the soul as never before.

Anyone who has experienced presence, either human or divine, will be able to meet the challenge of time, which is to stop trying to do the impossible either by escaping from the person one has been or by pretending to make over the person one will be. One should be neither obsessed by the past nor over-curious about the future. Forgiveness is not in our hands, and hope is not either. "The only genuine hope is hope in what does not depend on ourselves." Through prayer, "the zone of hope", the religious man remains in the world of presence. "Looked at from the outside, patience reduces to passivity, and hope reduces to desire. Hope, which is not merely desire, consists in asserting that there is at the heart of being, beyond all data, beyond all inventories and all calculations, a mysterious principle which is in connivance with me, which cannot but will that which I will, if what I will deserves to be willed, and is in fact willed by the whole of my being." Hope is the recognition, not the desire, of an order of poetic justice, which is the order of fullness and presence, which *is* "in connivance" with me. And however one gets in touch with this order or is moved by it, whether in experience of communion with other people, or in more strictly religious experiences, one has entered the land or zone of poetic justice where two worlds meet. "The zone of hope is prayer" and without hope our relation to the future is but scared desire. The zone of hope is also fidelity (as Conrad, as well as Marcel, understood it), for hope is not only beyond desire, it is a confirmation of our right to be charit-able. "Hope is not only a protestation inspired by love, but a sort of call, too, a desperate appeal to an ally who is himself also love."

By now the metaphysics behind the first part of the tale of The Sleeping Beauty should have emerged. The first part is a world of promise and hope, taking place in the morning, of giving and joy, taking place in the afternoon, but also of discontent and a falling away from the good world. Marcel has said somewhere that the history of mankind began with a falling away, a catastrophe. And so the first part ends, with a catastrophe. First promise and joy, then partial fulfilment because of a failing to provide; first joy and then hatred, threats, and the fulfilment of the threats. This is a world where both virtue and its counterparts triumph alternately, each with effects as real as the other. It is also a world of clear contraries, out of which magic and enchantment arise. Or were they there all along? The frog's prophecy competes with the thirteenth Wise Woman's, and hers again with the twelfth Wise Woman's. We are not told nor can we guess the power that they speak for. That the king and queen should have left their daughter at all is beyond understanding. Magic alone can reveal it. That the child should sleep on the edge of fulfilment again bewilders us; magic alone can account for it. And that she should not sleep for ever we cannot confirm, but magic may. And not only she but all the great court; this is beyond experience, and yet magic makes it easy for us to accept.

We too must be enchanted in order to cross the guard-ropes of experience. We too may be in touch with an order of life beyond experience which resembles the realm of desire but represents the region of hope. We may be, and we also may not be. We will not be able to confirm or deny this second order of nature as long as we stay with the first part. To those who lived through the years from the frog's prophecy to the year when the court fell asleep, life must have been full of surprises, so full of the extremes of joy and absurdity, of deserving and giving, of taking away, that no extension or reprieve could be imagined. That is how life is for those who live and die in such a time. Without the comfort of an extension of the known world, with its apparent luck and order and its unnecessary disorder, life will seem to be good or bad depending on one's own circumstances. Without history, without literature and art, without philosophy, all is chance. The world of experiences for those whose prospect is limited to what happened in the morning or afternoon is irrational or rational depending on what happens to them. The morning and afternoon do not make full sense by themselves; they seem to have everything: presents for the deserving and also for the undeserving, catastrophe for the good and indifferent alike. Morning and afternoon are the stuff of year by year history. But there is no enchantment in them, not in any of the scenes. There is a beginning of enchantment, but not its fullness. We do not yet believe all we see. It is a pleasing game, but not real. To be realized the night must come. In the day there are only *tableaux dormants*. There is charm and we are entertained, but we are not permanently affected. There is more to follow.

We do not believe yet in enchantment, but already we are used to the elements of its order. The order beyond probability is the order of presence. And in the morning there are presents, the manifestations of an order yet to be made completely intelligible. There is at first only disposability, gifts, and promises. In the twelfth Wise Woman one can see all three. But there is no mystery except for the observer with a sense of the future. The origin of the twelfth Wise Woman's powers is not known and nobody asks. She is dramatically acceptable and people are too interested in her intervention to wonder what right she has to speak. Everything is acceptable and nothing is understood; such is the way of the world.

What Marcel himself means by mystery is also still not enchantment. He too calls our attention to moral dispositions and their appearance. When he speaks of mystery or presence, he is mainly thinking of the inexhaustible fidelity of God towards us, which we, the only beings who can make and keep promises, need to imitate if we are not to die. His inexhaustibility is that of God's love, not man's knowledge. For him presence means a you who is near us, attentive and attending, a you on whom we can continually count. He does not seem to have in mind nor does he conjure up an enchantment which says: "In knowing you I am in touch with everything." This experience of noetic fullness is quite different from Marcel's moral readiness-without-limit. His world is the apparent world we are used to, of good things and bad, of deserving and giving, of withholding and threatening. If the centre of fidelity is God, the centre may seem far from us, so far that we are not ordinarily mystified or enchanted by the reality of His presence. Real enchantment appears quite otherwise; real enchantment annihilates time. Man forgets or ignores or is indifferent to all that surrounds. Real enchantment means time stops and a new music and life begin. This turning-point can be malevolent as well as beneficent. For the princess it was not bad; for those outside the castle, for the citizens in their cottages, it was very bad. They were left without memory. In any age when beauty sleeps, when nihilism is the usurper, enchantment will be agonizing rather than hopeful; it will keep us warm for the fullness of time, but it will also frustrate and lure to death. For most people, at such a time, there will be no enchantment, just life as one can bear it from one day through its night to the next day. For most people there will be no hope, no longing, no despair or surrender either; there will be many little achievements, many little failures and much frustration.

For those who view part one of the fairy tale or Marcel's writings, enlightenment is in store. However blind or indifferent or bewildered before, now we can recognize the features of our experience. In the face of our world, enchantment is shy. The kind of mystery, ethical rather than epistemological that Marcel calls us to, precedes the enchantment we are later immersed in. Marcel's kind of presence is presence as it appears in a dying world; we are introduced to it; we see it as desirable;

we see that without it, in its absence, life is empty, harsh, absurd. Where there is no permanence there is no constancy, only sham and disaster. So far we can understand the role of presence, but we do not feel its fullness. We see the enchantment appear on the stage, but we do not recognize ourselves on the stage. Through the morning and the afternoon we see the importance of presence, but we are not lifted from one order of experience to another. We may be persuaded, enlightened, but we do not yet believe. This is a real distinction, which for some people will seem to be only between the sorry way things are and the way they ought to be. It may, however, be more real than that. It is just possible that there is an order of justice beyond the order of experience, the features of which every morally-minded man knows so well. The first clue to it, if it exists, would be found in our understanding promise and giving as we know them to be, namely, although rudimentary and shaky, so important that we suspect their role is to advertise an order where both justice and justification come true. In the land of poetic justice princes and princesses attend each other, and their vision and joy spread throughout their kingdom. Two are alone, and away from them flows everything worthwhile. When one is alone, joy shrinks to madness.

In English "mystery" spells enchantment (and vulgarly, "teasing"). There is a moral mystery in part one of The Sleeping Beauty and in Marcel's philosophy: we see a promising and a fulfilling beyond the explanations given. But we accept this mystery; we are not mystified by it. The elements of this order concern an active morality, not inwardness or contemplation. In this order the saving sacrament, communion, is not the exploration by one person of another, of their mutual world, but practical co-operation. Each co-operative undertaking furthers the journey through the world or to paradise. Only in this sense is our vision in part one of The Sleeping Beauty or in Marcel raised above the requirements of this observable world.

We are not really concerned with the Rilkian "witnessing to the spiritual"; the accent is quite different. Rilke and Marcel are really far apart, not in interest but in practice. There is something emphatically dramatic and of the historical in Marcel and in the first part of the fairy tale; our human shape lies spread in clearest silhouette. Marcel's metaphysic of presence, mystery, and fidelity may tell us what has gone wrong with the world, what is missing from it, but his explorations often seem to be undertaken clinically rather than lovingly, with scalpel rather than with fingers. And perhaps that is the way it must be: enlightenment has to precede enchantment.

And is he not right, after all, as he tests the edges of our broken world, in suggesting that the real need is to infuse piety? Private and sentimental as this sounds, is it not what is missing, a piety broadly conceived towards the possibilities of fullness which man is being tendered? Whatever the pretended subject of the sentiment of piety (or fullness or presence), man would be submitting to a larger and more insistent being, larger than the ego, which in fact offers to overcome the ego and its fragile instinct for self-preservation and self-concern.

To live in or near the sentiment of presence or fullness, is in fact to live in or near an enchantment. And he who realizes the meaning of an enchantment will not die in the thorn hedge. But if one disregards or makes no attempt to understand the importance of enchantment, if one is only concerned about shoving aside obstacles and grabbing the prize, then the enchantment itself will viciously repel intruders. One must wait until it is time. What we look for is eternal, even if it is embedded in time and its wealth. So, too, Marcel would say, was Christ the Real Presence embedded.

2—EVENING AND NIGHT

"But round about the castle there began to grow a hedge of thorns,
    which every year became higher,
        and at last grew close up round the castle and all over it,
            so that there was nothing of it to be seen,
                not even the flag upon the roof.
But the story of the beautiful sleeping 'Briar-rose',
    for so the princess was named,
went about the country,
        so that from time to time Kings' sons came
        and tried to get through the thorny hedge into the castle.
But they found it impossible,
    for the thorns held fast together,
        as if they had hands,
and the youths were caught in them,
could not get loose again,
and died a miserable death."

A FREE SPIRIT

In the past hundred years man has had to think about questions which had never pressed upon him before. It may not be possible to say whether this period of questioning has already come to an end. The questions have, like questions in other times, become instinctive. And yet one can see here and there already men who are no longer obsessed by some of the obstacles that held up men not many years ago. We may speak fairly of three kinds of thinkers who represent three stages in the development of attitudes towards the barriers confronting man; in terms of the tale of Sleeping Beauty they are: those who assaulted the hedge too soon and were caught, those who watched the example of the assaulters and waited, those who, in the fullness of time, believed they need wait no longer. Nietzsche, the chief of the free spirits, is an example of the first; Heidegger, the shepherd of being, of the second. At the present time aggressiveness, caution, and faith all have their followers. And yet from the point of view of the latter, the men of faith, both aggressiveness and caution are untimely. From the point of view of the former, caution is unnecessary and faith craven. From the point of view of caution, aggressiveness is foolhardy and faith a misconception. To put this in a nineteenth century way, denying God, waiting for God, longing for God are all observable, verifiable experiences. But is awakening God verifiable? The man of faith says it is. But is it verifiable in the same way that his longing is? The man who waits for God has an advantage over the others that they do not appreciate; he does not perish in the thorn hedge and he can believe in God without believing in the time or the way. But the aggressive man wins or loses in one throw, and the man of faith may not know enough to distinguish miracle from mirage. The man who believes can reply to the man who waits that if life is waiting only, he will never know enough to recognize God if he does become present. The recognition of Presence depends on the prior experience of presences.

For those living in the one hundred years during which the castle slept, life was no more questionable than before. But this only means that most lives at any time are lived without inner turbulence, unless their owners fall victim to overpowering misfortune. Most people do not have enough historical sensitiveness to know that their time and themselves differ from the past, though presumably they feel that their own time is more convenient. From the past century one must accept Nietzsche as a prime sample of the spirited confidence of the very middle class which he abhorred, a sample who understood the weakness of his age and embodied its daring. Like Marx he stood for a strand of honesty and hope that separated itself from the commonplaces and complacency of the time. Whatever the historical and ideological connections between Nietzsche's anger against mediocrity and Marx's against dehumanization, it is clear now that both the spokesman for individualism and the spokesman for socialism thought they had to re-examine everything. They could accept nothing; they questioned everything. Their own answers may strike us now as being too simple even for their questions. We should be more impressed at the unanimity of their mode of answering. For when Nietzsche spoke of "creating values", and Marx of recognizing the direction of history, they were not expressing opposite points of view. Marx's direction was known only to himself; and the simplified version of society which it pointed to was just as innocent as the individualistic utopia of Nietzsche. The latter assumed that all would be as it should be if the gifted and exceptional were free and busy. The former assumed that everyone would be happy if everyone owned what everyone else owned. That both should have thought that the evils of the world could be reduced or put out of mind merely by bringing about one and only one kind of freedom, indicates a simplicity and confidence and one-sidedness that strikes one to-day as belonging to a simpler and more easy century.

Nietzsche replied to the indifference of the middle class to exceptional individuals by being indifferent to the fate of that class in a society ruled by exceptional individuals. Marx extended the middle-class, overwhelming belief in justification by property by advocating the extension of property to everyone. Each was a child of his time. And yet each, paradoxically, had the kind of social consciousness that was so badly needed, each working for a different, but equally neglected segment of the population. These prophets of a better, nobler world equally believed that the old world and its trumped-up God were dead, and that man alone could answer the questions and make the answers come true which a God had formerly been used for. In this they were ahead of most of their time, and like Stendhal, belonged to "the happy few". How happy they were, is hard to tell. They suffered much for their doctrine.

Marx could join Nietzsche in saying: "My time has not yet come; some people are born posthumously."

The posthumous prophet is a homeless soul, and it is in irony only that we can think of him as one of the happy few. His anonymity in his own time was overpowering enough to have crushed lesser men. Only by an equally powerful expression of his ideas is he able to make his contemporaries notice him at all. In this Marx was much more successful than Nietzsche, for the former attached himself to the working class movements of Europe which tried to hasten the day of final revolution in the middle of the century. Each had loyal friends, and Marx an unbelievably long-suffering wife. Each knew from abortive experiences that the century could not be deflected from its course. Nietzsche, the more sensitive of the two by far, understood their situation and, prophetically, the situation of the twentieth century, as that of homelessness. "We homeless ones . . . we children of the future . . . how could we be at home in the present?" How could they indeed, in a century which admired only the individualism of the *entrepreneur* (in every profession), the collectivism of convention. They were homeless simply because they were untimely, "children of the future". They could, without a doubt, have been as much at home in their own time as the rest, for it was a time of great inner security and comfort, despite the progress of a century of industrialization, discovery, intellectual probing. But they were, as Nietzsche continues, "unfavourable to all ideals which could make us feel at home in this frail, broken-down transition period". Can a man be happy whose ideals run counter to those of his age, and who sees clearly that his age is already dissolving into a new, unknown, simpler if harsher age? Nietzsche and Marx both, grimly, thought not. They knew soon enough that they were sacrificial victims. Unlike religious prophets they could not take comfort from the nearness of a presence on whose behalf they had spoken. They were speaking on behalf of a future known only to them and not experienced by anyone. We recall that Nietzsche always disclaimed that he himself was a superman. He did not indulge in that kind of wishful thinking. He only claimed that he knew more than other men of his time, not that he was capable of more.

What he knew was that the old God was dead. One might think that this knowledge would not distinguish him from the many "enlightened" men of the nineteenth century who, like Stendhal or Mill, never had a God to lose. But Nietzsche realized two things that the others did not. He saw that civilization was already depending on the efforts of man rather than on a belief in another order of effort, and that when men understood how much on their own they were, they would feel homeless. If they were strong, they would welcome this knowledge as the opening of new horizons towards which they could sail. The seas would be free at last. Only Nietzsche and Dostoyevsky saw fully the fact and the consequences of the death of God. And they both understood that if God died it was not because he had become sick, but because man no longer needed him and murdered him. Ivan Karamazov muses: "We only need to destroy the idea of God in man . . . and everything will begin anew. Men will unite to take from life all it can give, but only for joy and happiness in the present world. Man will be lifted up with a spirit of divine Titanic pride, and the man-god will appear. Everyone will know he is mortal and will accept death proudly and serenely like a God. He will love his brother without need of reward." Dostoyevsky himself—and Ivan—did not believe all this, but he understood that the time had come when men did and could believe it. The fact that he did not believe and Nietzsche did, is the best possible proof of the availability of the knowledge of God's death to anyone at the end of the last century. There is no difference between Dostoyevsky's fiction and Nietzsche's prophecy; each is both prophecy and fiction, each is intensely serious and important to its author. First deny God, a transcendent order, and then you may do as you like. Or as Dostoyevsky said elsewhere: "Everything is lawful."

The death or denial of God was the denial of an order of presence or justice transcending individual effort. Dostoyevsky, who understood the consequences differently from Nietzsche, realized that if you deny transcendence, you deny presence, for presence is the appearance of something unique and other than oneself which while offering itself demands recognition. He pointed out, dramatically, that the man who denied God was incapable of love. Such a man either turned selfish or morally paralysed. To-day it is fashionable to say, repeating an old story, that morality does not depend on religion. This may be, but what Dostoyevsky saw, which Nietzsche was unable to see, was that if you deny presence *or* a God who is Presence, you are psychologically incapable of interest in or commerce with the presence of other human beings or nature. He himself could not believe in the utter transcendence of an Explainer God, remote from the contradictions of life and reason. And he supposed that God, if there was a God, was in some way present in and through the world, waiting to be acknowledged and communed with. To what extent Dostoyevsky's God was pantheistic is a question that only very careful scrutiny of his writings and an intimate knowledge of Orthodoxy could answer. That he identified this present God with the figure of Christ cannot, however, be denied. The interest for us in all this comes from the adjustment he obviously was making to the prevailing rationalistic conception of a God who should explain suffering but who was too remote to. Dostoyevsky answers the rationalist and himself by postulating a God who is Presence. If you can believe in Presence, you can believe in God and the incomprehensibility of his connection with free men who misuse their freedom and then ask for explanations. You can believe in Presence if you have encountered presences, in the guise of persons and nature. You can encounter them as presences and allow them to see you as something more than an enigma, only if you admit the existence of a world which is based on Presence. The interconnection of God and morality in Dostoyevsky must be understood in this way.

Nietzsche saw it quite differently. He was willing to accept the dictum, "Everything is lawful", simply because he had never had a belief that Presence was more important than Ego. Nietzsche persuades only when he appeals to one's appreciation of the sacredness of the Ego. Even his conception of friendship was one-sided; he wanted recognition. He had no notion of the need or the pleasure of giving. Therefore he could not understand what would happen to a civilization built on egoism rather than on presence. With his great individuals of the future encouraged and provided for, what, he asks naïvely and callously, could go wrong? Marx, likewise, had asked what could possibly go wrong if everyone had a share in the ownership of the means of production? Dostoyevsky never committed this nineteenth-century simplicity; he knew that life could not be reduced and explained by panaceas. For him the crisis of civilization was a crisis of presence and absence, encounters and alienations. His great heroes were always alienated men who longed for a presence they had lost touch with or never had long enough to remember clearly. They all understood that the problem of God and the problem of love or friendship or law were inseparable because they both were the problem of presence, seen in different dimensions.

Nietzsche, on the other hand, was as sure of his own importance and the sufficiency of others like him or greater than he, as sure of this sufficiency as he was sure of the disappearance of the order of transcendent beings. What he did not see was that man is not and cannot be sufficient or happy by himself. That he himself was not, one can put down to lack of the recognition he deserved. But his progressive alienation from everything that was real, from nature as well as persons, is at least a symbol of a progressively narrow content of consciousness in a man who thought he did not need an order of presence. For the most effectual mode of presence is its mutuality. One cannot be aware of some one as present without being aware that gift asks for gift in return. If one does not see this, the stream of giving itself dries up. All that Nietzsche could see was that there was no real, transcendent hindrance any more to great men, sensitive, intelligent men, doing and saying and thinking what they pleased and could. Had he understood the conception of God or presence or love that Dostoyevsky wrote about in novel after novel, he might have lost heart. For however he would have judged presence had he understood it, whether or not he would have believed in a God who was Present, he would at any rate have realized that he had failed to understand something he claimed to understand, in reality as in Dostoyevsky.

Both Nietzsche and Dostoyevsky put the denial of God in the mouths of madmen. Ivan Karamazov was distracted, suffering from brain fever, when his hallucinatory devil reminded him that all men had to do to be happy was to deny God. Kirillov, who had proved to himself that man would be God if he denied God, was also mad. Nietzsche was not yet mad when he wrote of the madman who cried in the market place: "I seek God. Whither is God? I shall tell you. We have killed him, you and I. We are all murderers . . . God is dead." It needed some kind of madness to escape the complacency of the nineteenth century long enough to see what was around the corner. It needed an alienation which could recognize, and rejoice in, alienation. It needed sacrificial victims who would have to be caught in a thorn hedge to warn mankind of the real perils of a belief in self-sufficiency. Nietzsche himself had some understanding of his role as a victim, but not clearly enough to teach himself the saving doctrine and drama that Dostoyevsky wrote of. He read Dostoyevsky without seeing in him anything more than a great "psychologist".

That God is dead is good news only if you have never believed in God. This was not the reception men have at other times given to similar pronouncements. We recall that occasion Plutarch tells of, in the time of the Emperor Tiberius, when a man travelling on a coasting ship on the way to Italy from Greece heard a voice from the shore call out: "Tell the people at Palodes that Great Pan is dead." And when the ship reached Palodes, they called out as instructed: "Great Pan is dead," and heard from the people great groaning and lamentation. Great Pan is said to have died when Christ was born, and by some he was missed. This is a legend, and expresses sentiment rather than fact. It is like another legend which the Greeks still tell, of the nereids who stop ships and ask: "Does King Alexander live?" And if the answer is: "He lives and reigns," they let it proceed, otherwise they destroy it. Great Pan and Alexander were mourned. Nietzsche's legend does not have a place for the mourning of Christ, unless it be his ironic suggestion that Requiem Masses be said for the dead God. Great Pan was mourned, and yet he brought panic to all those who met him alive. Those who have read Kenneth Grahame's *The Wind in the Willows* will recall his charming and persuasive picture of Pan, the Presence in Nature, who both desolates and renews. Pan is power, electrically quick, helping, laughing, belittling. No triviality can withstand his grin. He has too much energy, too much commonsense for shrunken souls; he shuts down their little vision as a fog does over a rowboat. And then the panic comes. But the reason men fear Pan is not the reason why they mourned for him. Only where Pan is, or where panic can arise, do men feel the vast billow of hollowness around them, which upsets and churns them. Men do not panic who have a present being to fall back on; Pan is such overwhelming presence that he reminds smaller presences of how very tiny they are. Men should be grateful for panic, if through it they can learn how empty they are. One is tempted to say that Pan was the forerunner of "the real presence, the prince of peace". But it may be more correct to say that if Christ has not died for ever neither has Pan, that what Christ is to the presence of persons, Pan is to the presence of nature.

Nineteen centuries after Tiberius's reign, "the real presence" was proclaimed dead. He had, it seemed, lived even longer than Pan. And again some mourned, but in secret, for in their hearts they knew men were tired of God and glad to get rid of him. They were particularly glad to get rid of God who had to be worshipped in degrading effigy. Let God die so that man can live. So said Nietzsche and Marx, the forerunners of the revolutionists of the present century. How similar is Rozanov's fable of the iron curtain to Nietzsche's of the madman in the market place. For if one is political and the other is religious, both express a cultural change that both individualist and socialist welcomed.

> "With a clang, a thud, and a bang the iron curtain
> is dropping down on Russian history.
>> The performance is over,
>> The public gets up.
>> 'It's time to put on our overcoats and go home.'
>> They look around.
>> But there are neither overcoats to put on,
>> nor houses to go to."

But what is the cultural change that Rozanov, as opposed to Nietzsche, saw? It is the desolation of homelessness without the hope of the open seas. It is the drabness that one now associates with the totalitarian states. So many have been made homeless, in fact and in nerve, since 1914; so many frontiers have been crossed by so many displaced persons, who have lost presence and home. Could Nietzsche still speak of the open seas? Could he still suppose that he was equipped to bequeath people homes? Not unless he learned in the meanwhile the connection between home and presence and justice. It is easier even now to see the desolateness in the political fable than in Nietzsche's mischievous blasphemy. There is something attractive as well as almost incredibly blind about Nietzsche's boasting. "For all those who somehow had a 'god' for company, what I know as solitude did not exist." Can a solitude be made bearable, to say nothing of exhilarating, by faith in one's own power and vision and destiny? Are we to assume cracks in Nietzsche's faith when we read: "We homeless ones", "what I know of solitude", and similar phrases? How much was he aware that his loneliness was due to something more than non-recognition, that it was due to sterility or refusal? For the former one may give pity, for the latter there is little excuse or comfort. It is the ambiguity of Nietzsche's motives that draws from us an ambiguous reply. We follow and yet condemn. How can one condone his saying: "Not to cleave to any person, be it even the dearest, every person is a prison and also a recess." And yet does not this sentence, which describes Nietzsche himself so fully, also describe the very alienation of the contemporary world? Do we follow Nietzsche only because he enlightens us about ourselves?

We view ironically his "good solitude, the free wanton lightsome solitude", because we know it was nothing of the kind even for him. Do we follow him only because in our understanding of his role we also pity him as a person? Or do we condemn him for letting his vision of ego refuse presence? Or may we suppose that presence was not offered him? Surely this is not possible for anyone living in the pleasant Alpine-Riviera scenery Nietzsche moved about in, who knew men and women both solicitous for his welfare and worth knowing for their own sake. He who said that "every profound spirit needs a mask" to protect itself from the interference of mediocre persons, himself had a mask which prevented him from falling in love with either persons or things. He loved only himself and his vision. If we do not blame him very much, it is because

Nietzsche always strikes those who know him well as rather innocent and childlike. But we ought to recognize that the world of masks, which is the world of theatricality, is also the world of madness which itself often looks childlike and innocent. We are all mad so long as we wear masks instead of faces. We say: "If the world does not want me, I will make my own world." Perhaps this is what Nietzsche was born to feel and say. He said, early in his career, of the Greeks that their cheerfulness, their inveterate cheerfulness, must have covered over much disgust. He reminds us that even the pleasantest fairy tale may be only a mask for suffering.

The tale of The Sleeping Beauty, which charms with its story of an awakening of beauty, a story of presence, may have come out of just such suffering and longing for a break through some thorn hedge in life. But he who knows he wears a mask, and who is not masquerading for fun, becomes isolated, sometimes to his complete and utter disorientation. This alienation is the fate that awaits individualists and free spirits who cannot acknowledge an order of presence. Those who have entered "the period of isolation" that Dostoyevsky said we must all pass through, may not be so fortunate as to leave behind their pride. They may remain with their causes and their illusions, to suffer the "strange new plague that had come to Europe from the depths of Asia". In this last dream of Raskolnikov, Dostoyevsky, prophetically, tells of the fate of those who suffer the plague of self-sufficiency. "All were to be destroyed, except a very few. . . . Never had men considered themselves so intellectual and so completely in possession of the truth as these sufferers. . . . Each thought that he alone had the truth. . . . They were a pure chosen people, destined to found a new race and a new life, to renew and purify the earth, but no one had seen these men, no one had heard their words or their voices." These Nietzschean "new barbarians" have been heard and seen and encountered very recently, and their words still seem new to millions of dispossessed, who suffer that they may be saved. But "the alarm bell was ringing all day long in the towns", and the rest of the world made jittery by the sound of the warning and the self-assurance. The plague did not arise in the depths of Asia, as Dostoyevsky foretold—nor has the star of Orthodoxy risen in the East again—but in central Europe from which it has now spread to Asia. The fairy court has gone to sleep behind a hedge which both protects its treasure of beauty, law, and presence, and prevents the plague-ridden men from knowing what they miss. There is little outside the plague area, except voices, to remind the plague-stricken what health and peace and comfort can be. Will a time come when prophecy can be fulfilled, and the right young man approach the hedge of thorns which will turn into roses? The only indications of that new time, that full time, are the voices, the story which is still read, and the nostalgia. Never have so many men considered themselves so completely in possession of the truth. Never have so many men been willing to immolate themselves for their conception of what is true. "Zarathustra . . . the greatest gift ever bestowed . . . the deepest book, born of the inmost fullness of truth . . . the veritable book of mountain air . . . a Goethe or a Shakespeare would not have been able to breathe for a moment in this terrific atmosphere of passion and elevation." How little different from the communist pride and simplicity is Nietzsche's egocentricity. "Why am I so clever?" "Why am I so wise?" Why indeed? Because you are plague-stricken. The hundred years of sleep have removed all natural resistance to this bacillus. Without the examples of presence, the authority and charity of the king and queen, the dutifulness of the court, the friendship of the Wise Women, the beauty and virtue of the king's daughter, without living presences, one is left to one's life of injustice, one's anger and eagerness for any kind of justice, one's willingness to sacrifice all to get a minimum for all.

Christ and Pan died, and men were left without the natural, incarnate reminders of presence in Person and Nature. A sacrament continued the first for those who could see the sameness in Person and sacrament; they became fewer as time went by. As long as men could see presence in a sacrament, they tended to ignore the presences of nature. Not until the Renaissance did men's interest in nature revive. And then men were more able for a time to see presence in nature than in the Eucharist. The English romantic poets raised this sensitivity to presences in nature to a very high level. Only since then, with the increasing dehumanization of life in cities, has the interest in sacraments, symbolism of all kinds, and the straight incarnation of presences in persons, been revived. For the first time since the Renaissance, men appreciate presences in both these elemental modes at the same time.

In modern times especially, presence of mind has been substituted for presence of person or nature. Cleverness, show, and success being the signs of effort, energy, and sufficiency, have replaced the fuller, more permanent presence. Presence of mind is too one-sided to satisfy a person aware of a world indifferent to single men among billions. Only where a community is small or where one narrows one's outlook so that the environment seems small, can presence of mind flourish without looking comic. Only in a world which is assured of the material world turning out as right as the world of the spirit—an eighteenth-century world, let us say—does presence of mind have a place that can be admired. But this is a limited world, and easily destroyed by the many pressures of modern life that humble the individual mind to the point where it is alienated rather than present. Shall we return to this kind of presence? Only if it is humbled to meet the total demands of presence in the person as a whole. It is not presence of mind which carried the prince through the thorn hedge, but it was the assumption of just such a presence which immolated one free spirit after another before the time was right for the true prince to walk through.

There is an illusion of presence as well as a reality; presence of mind is imitation presence. There is an illusion, a groping after presence, which more sensitive persons, particularly artists and writers, have tried to recover in the present century. One cannot help wondering whether part of Henry James's mysteriousness and part of his persistent failure is not that he and his characters are continually groping after presences that they have never fully experienced. There is something just as pathetic in James's characters failing time and again to communicate even to each other or James in his prefaces to his readers, as in Nietzsche's pretended Dionysiac vision. There is an imitation presence as well as a substitute for presence. Which enlightens us more? Which is more pathetic?

Presence is not easily caught. She is mimicked at our peril. The princess, with her beauty dormant, is the quiet, central power-house of authority, familiarity, approval, love, and permanence. We cannot possess her; she must recognize us and possess us. She is not there for the taking but for the touching. No man has what it takes to get her. She is there for the giving, the awakening. We must awaken presence so that we may be given it. We are lost if we assault beauty in her thorny nest. Just so, in that dying, complacent century, were the free spirits caught. They could not loosen themselves once they had embroiled themselves, and they died miserably. Why such misery? They had not murdered persons, only a God. They had not violated, only assaulted. They had pretended knowledge and strength, and it turned out they did not know the time or the way. They did not even have energy to extricate themselves. Do we pity them perhaps because we suspect they were victims to some extent of a time when no one could succeed who had not the childhood memory, as Newman or Dostoyevsky, of some good presence? Perhaps they really deserved to break through the hedge. Does the present recognition make up for their posthumousness? Does their alienation canonize them because they symbolized the alienated age that has followed them? This alienation between man's deserving and man's consciousness of an order of justice transcending his petty, cruel efforts, is so comfortably mirrored in "the happy few" who died so poorly over half a century ago, long before the hedge had begun to flower.

They are not mere victims, for their immolation makes some sense to us. They bear the flaw of presumption and are crowned with our thorns. But they triumph in our pity and in our admiration for more energy than we have left, save in sheer self-defence, collectively conceived and administered. If they had not died, we should be so clever, so wise. We too might have to wait for the fullness of time; we too might understand that we are not the central figures. This is just what Heidegger does understand, and this is why he waits. For he believes that presence is still far away, but perhaps on the way back to us. He will not confuse himself or his time with the true prince who walked through the briars unhurt. He thinks this too is no time for heroics, but for patience and receptivity. He wishes to learn Nietzsche's lesson well. But he may be wrong. If there is no hero, there may be a heroine asleep and at no distance at all. And the time may be nearer too than Heidegger thinks. What would its sign be? Does he know? Will anyone know who has not been chosen? There are those who deserve and those who have the power to give, and the latter have this power because it has been given to them. The princess only sleeps—does God sleep too?—the youths have died because they disturbed her.

Entrapped in the hedge, they could not get loose. The hedge had more hands than they. Why were these brave men not rescued? Had they so alienated themselves from their fellows that no one knew their real plight? They had despised their fellows themselves, and even out of pity their friends and relations were helpless before their withdrawal. They lived and died alone. To return to life would have been to return on the terms of those they rejected because they underestimated them. They preferred the final loneliness of pride and aggressiveness to the humbleness of admitting they too had misjudged and were weak. They had wanted to be freer than any before them. They had wanted to crush freedom as a man crushes his loved one. Their own beauty was the freedom they inspired in others. Unable to love, they awakened a dormant sympathy and love in those whom they had belittled. They were nihilists, self-confessed, and victims born for a sacrifice in a time that knew no sacraments. Born out of time, before even their time, they now remind us of the fullness of time.

They remind us, but not their contemporaries, who pitied because they were all-too-human, not because they understood. And these revolutionaries, socialists and individualists alike, still die for a cause they have simplified below the level of human need. And while their plague runs its course, the world waits, not daring to ask for what has already been so plainly rejected. But already the waiting world is saying that there may be a sleeping beauty to be awakened, there may be a fullness of time. Those who wait are the hardest of all to pity, for they may be on the edge of discovery. In that case they will receive their reward. Or they may be indolent and proud of their inactivity, knowing they are incapable of discovery. In that case, they will be despised. They are waiting for the meaning and the presence to appear. Like Simone Weil, they will press only when they feel the pressure around them yield of its own accord. They are not convinced that presence is hitched to deserving. They are wrong, but who of us dares to admonish them? Have we climbed the mountain to the thorn hedge near the summit? Have we looked down from the castle roof to the free spirits in the hedge or their successors waiting outside?

Who of us even guessed that there was always a mountain to climb before we could reach the castle? Kafka did, and he did not believe much in presence. Did we know that those waiting must sit in snow and cold, mist and wind, the climate of a Europe and Asia homeless with the ruins of two great wars? Warmed only occasionally by the bright alpine sun, those who wait have the advantage of consistency over those of us who are in a hurry to be given what our ancestors could not take. Did we think the castle situated in the valley, or in some flat-land? But the castle is on high, a mountain must be climbed even to see the thorn hedge. The hedge must flower. Are we, to quote Kafka, "reserved for a great Monday"? And is it true that "Sunday will never end"? Will the twilight of the idols of sufficiency end, and the Great Noon and Great Monday come for those who wait? A hundred years of Sundays must pass before that dawn appears? And who can measure one hundred years? Does it begin every time a man is born?

A SHEPHERD OF BEING

Like the noble youths who died in the briars, like Christ who was crowned with thorns, Nietzsche in his madness accepted his fate as "the crucified". The irony of his passing was that he had prefaced his famous words, "God is dead", by the less noticed, "I seek God". He was hardly conscious of the irony, for he himself was glad God had died. Had he not helped to kill him? He killed God so that man could live once again. This was his metaphysical struggle against true Christianity and Platonism, against a transcendent order. But while objecting to Christianity, he despised Christendom, the form of decadence of the modern world. In this moral struggle against his time he, like Kierkegaard, hit out at those who called themselves Christians falsely. Men "no longer knew what it meant to be a Christian; Christendom had triumphed over Christ." And

Nietzsche agreed with Kierkegaard. But unlike Kierkegaard, he believed in a form of self-sufficiency, a will to power, which made true Christianity unnecessary. Instead of looking for truth, Nietzsche wished to create truth.

That he stated certain critical truths, critical of his time, there is no doubt. But that he brought into the world any new principle of existence, there is every doubt. In him many old strands of individualism, chosen from Greece, Rome, Italy, and Germany, were woven into a theory of energy and consciousness by which the strong-minded could be guided. But if they were to be led only to the euphoria, depression, and final alienation of Nietzsche himself, what value this culmination of individualisms? Whether Nietzsche was a sacrifice or just a bad example for other men to avoid, we need not try to decide. Certainly, as an illustration for a fairy tale, he had his effect on other men. For towards the end of the one hundred years' sleep, other noble youths began to hesitate to assault the thorn hedge without testing the thorns' sharpness first. No longer did they cry so brassily that God was dead. They recognized that prickly death awaited any who imagined that the test of their freedom—or their own divinity—lay in immolation. We notice now how subdued in contrast to the energetic individualists of the past century are Heidegger, Kafka, Proust, Joyce. They do not wear themselves out rebelling against their time, transition figures though they may be between Nietzsche and a figure like Marcel. If they were isolated and have become figures as well as authors, is it not because they were victims of the several new pressures of the twentieth century, and not because they broke themselves in combat with their time? They withdrew instead of fighting, and in this sense, Mr. Martin Turnell is right when he says they are prisoners rather than outsiders. But the prisoners are overshadowed by the outsiders, whom they still respect and whose fate they fear. In Heidegger especially we can see the consequences of this respect for the free spirit of Nietzsche. For instead of proclaiming that God is dead, Heidegger says that God has withdrawn. Instead of denying God, Heidegger—with many others—waits for him to return.

Those who follow Heidegger's philosophical career know that he is an illuminating example of those who wait for God, because he has consistently sought one thing only all his life, the disclosure of Being. His philosophical studies, abetting his disposition, convinced him that the more mankind philosophized, the less capable men became of conceiving the difference between beings and Being. Heidegger saw his role almost in terms of Nietzsche's madman, who, while recognizing that God was absent, pretended to be seeking God. The difference seems to be that Heidegger really has been seeking Being, while proclaiming the absence of man's concern with it. He has been seeking Being for at least thirty years, and he has sought it where it was lost, in man, the shepherd of Being, in human subjectivity, in the dread of death that remained when God's presence was withdrawn. In making men see the nothingness in and about man, Heidegger hoped, by contrast, to help men imagine the reality and presence which prevent a natural sense of reality from subsiding into complete indifference. Heidegger has been badly misunderstood, partly because he has distracted men by his brief but shameful association with the Nazis, partly because he employs neologisms, and partly because of the intrinsic difficulty of his aim. Unfortunately his critics, who have not been so impressed by Nietzsche's words "God is dead" as Heidegger has, and who ignore the homelessness of our time that both Nietzsche and Heidegger have called attention to, would have us refuse to hear him at all. It should not be so easy to be ignorant of the homelessness of our time. The great Wars Nietzsche foretold have come; subjectivism and relativism thrust themselves and their neuroses on us and our friends every day. Only here and there is anything at all said about an order of justice—must it be poetic?—which transcends the defence of security and liberty.

The peoples of the world are separable now as always into those who have suffered much and those who have not. The complacency of the latter still dominates both politics and everyday life, even though the discomfort of the former has already persuaded millions to put up with an order of slavery to the State or to some cause. Henry James's phrase, "excursion into chaos", fittingly tells of the emotional and physical character of the past thirty-five years for half or more of the peoples of the earth. This chaos is the new chaos of the displaced or homeless person. How can one feel a person at all if displaced or homeless? Many have had to ask this, and have had to admit that without some pretence of place, of belonging, they could not exist as persons. The question still is open as to what place is best, what home should be like. The provisional answer is that any place is better than none.

After the first war, refugees were sometimes called "stateless persons". This inhumane phrase did not survive the second war. The words that have replaced "stateless" are not only varied, they are more personal. Men are not stateless, they are estranged, alienated, enslaved, orphaned, exiled, isolated, thwarted, disquieted, and so on. Whether extended or not, it is an appalling vocabulary which almost everyone uses to characterize acquaintances as well as foreigners. Perhaps never before could an historian come across the fact of so many millions of men and women forced to think of themselves as foundlings who could resent their state. When men cease to take evils for granted, they learn all the degrees of dehumanization they can go through. The orphans, then, no longer believe some men have to be orphans. They have had their inborn instinct for home recognized by parties and governments; many of them can even remember former homes, for not all have been born in exile.

There is an exile of the nerves as well as of the body, an exile for the intellectual and for the ordinary man as well as for the politically unwanted. No matter what the immediate cause of exile, wandering, disorientation, the world is to-day much more conscious of alienation than in any time in history. There may be no more alienation, but there are more kinds and more awareness of them. It is becoming harder to go about one's business, ignoring the press and unease in the world and in those one lives with. Even in the country it is harder to sit unmindful of tasks, obstacles, threats. The birds sing, the fog rolls in and out as usual, pictures are painted, gardens are grown, but unease remains in one's bones like malaria. One rids oneself of the cause of some unease, thinking that now peace will come for a time, but the habit of disquietude, or some other cause, prevents one from relaxing. "We are the last to have known such things," said Rilke, thinking, superficially at least, of the aristocratic amenities of Europe, but probably also of the slower pace, the assurance of merit being recognized, of effort growing undisturbed in congenial climate. And Rilke, like Nietzsche, died almost as Shestov would have men die. "The best death is really the one which is considered the worst: to die alone, in a foreign land, in a poor-house, or, as they say, like a dog under a hedge. Then at least one may spend one's last moments honestly." But it is better to die outside the hedge than in it, better still to die waiting outside the hedge than in the flat-land below where hearts are dead. Why better? Because those who died in the hedge itself can waste their time blaming the hedge for the aggression that was their own pride's making.

Our time is, despite its critical, historical wisdom, impoverished, not only because God is still dead but because dying men seldom are trained to admit their last loneliness. And those who do will be tempted to see their solitude not as a part of their unsigned compact with life but as a consequence of the age they were put by accident in. Our time is impoverished, not only like other times when men thought of this world as a passageway to a better or worse one, but because we can no longer see it in terms of a journey at all. We are merely here or there, not on the way anywhere. Our civilization not only "lacks clarity about grief, death, and love", as Heidegger has recently said; it lacks the spirit to sustain purposes and promises. This is what is so alarming; even the man who theorizes seriously, believingly, about promises is as likely as the next one to break promises to someone who no longer matters to him. The smallest moral balance, honesty, is ebbing away. When that goes completely, "everything is lawful" at last.

Heidegger had claimed that "the characteristic of this age consists in the reservation of the dimension of the holy". With God dead or withdrawn, man is really on his own. The consequences are, from almost anyone's point of view, desolating. But not everyone agrees that this is the cause. If God, or the Holy, or Being, is reserved, does that mean that, as with the sacrament reserved on an altar, God is waiting, rather than man, for man to approach? Or does this mean that God reserves the right to stay away until man finds out how much he needs Him? In the meantime much of life is spent in waiting for things that never come, for things we fear, and things we desire. And much of life is spent waiting for things which do come and which turn out to be unimportant, means rather than ends. Much of life is spent in anticipation of something we cannot even define, but which the premonitory ache of nostalgia advises us to wait around for. But no one can live in the flat-lands on waiting alone; one must work and be entertained, plan and achieve. Unless one waits outside the hedge for the fullness of time—unless one withdraws from others and imitates in a twentieth century way the more violent isolation of the past, one will not understand the difference between the confidence that one can advance, of the last hundred years, and the disposition to share with others whatever comes, that characterizes the present.

Only those near some kind of voluntary isolation themselves will understand the hope that inspired Nietzsche when he said: "We who wait as it were on the mountains twixt to-day and to-morrow . . . we the premature children of the coming century . . . we prefer much rather to live on mountains apart and out of season." For there, in "a voluntary retirement into a region of ice and mountain peaks—the search for all that is strange and questionable in existence" takes place, while below the life of routines, the life without consciousness of history, goes on. But no longer are those in the mountain huts ready to assault the hedge and take by force what is not their fortune to receive. They know their limitations; they know that there is a fullness of time, which will be known first of all to those waiting for dawn on the peaks. But if there is something comic or pathetic about Heidegger, one of the most renowned philosophers of modern times, living away from cities in a ski hut, we may see a more dismaying spectacle than this, the true prince passing through the thorn hedge while Heidegger keeps protesting that the time has not come. This is the risk he takes. Like the man in Kafka's parable in *The Trial* who waited outside the door to the Law until at death the door which was meant for him was shut in his face, Heidegger too may wait too long.

Although a free spirit could approach the hedge in the twilight of the idols, Heidegger, the shepherd of being, has to sit it out during the night that follows. He has admitted that we can only approach Being or the Holy in the evening, in "Abendland" (never "the West" or "the Occident," but always "Evening Land"). Our eyes are not strong enough to see the sun; like the fugitives from Plato's cave, we must begin with reflections in the water at night. We approach the gods in their dimming, which is our darkness. So "this period of gloom", as Nietzsche called it, need not require despair. One is sad because one is incapable of naming Being, but one has a lesson learned from the past to make one wait for the long night to pass and the new day to dawn. How close then Heidegger is to Nietzsche, how much more severely he appraises the task of those who have climbed the mountain, above complacency and subjectivity. How much more clearly he has defined the nature of man, which man no longer believes in, as Existence, a standing away or surpassing of what one is born with. Man, the pointer to being, man, the "creature of distance", must and can surpass himself and his immediate environment in order to remain human. Only man can communicate, can travel, can make new things, can go beyond himself. Only man can come back again to his beginning. The creature of distance is he who is present to another also, who has regard for and interest in other beings. In the distance is the mystery of being which Heidegger as well as Marcel now writes of, which is open to man only once he has opened himself expectantly to the Being which employs him as shepherd.

The latest descendant of Nietzsche is the atheistic existentialism of Sartre. For him, "everything is lawful" to one who chooses boldly. Heidegger is right in protesting that he and Sartre have nothing in common. For Heidegger has learned from Nietzsche's defeat, while Sartre repeats it. Once again the aggressive man proclaims an individualism in which love is thought to be a prison. But Sartre has rejected not only love, God, and mediocre men, he has deliberately rejected nature too. And if he claims that no man can be fully free unless all men are free, he is merely emphasizing the importance of isolation to a life of self-interest. Let me alone and I am human; interfere with me, and I lose myself. But what is this self which draws nothing from anyone or anything outside it, which makes itself heard but needs nothing? Is this not the self that assaults the thorn hedge, proclaiming an understanding of the quest for The Absolute but pretending to care only for little absolutes? And what are these little absolutes Sartre cares for? Is there a world of things, places, people, he is nostalgic for when away from them? To what or whom does he give himself when at home? Or has he rejected home altogether, like Nietzsche, who found home only when taken there mad?

We must know something of these different stages in the passing of Nietzsche's individualism. The only thing that will distinguish the true prince's confidence from the shut-in assurance of the egoists will be his knowledge of their trials, their limitations. He too must know what it is to be free, and what it is to be obsessed by a freedom indistinguishable from self-enclosure. He must have heard of those who attacked before it was time and were imprisoned. He must know also of the bored but busy life in the flat-land, where people no longer look up to see the mountain on which the castle stands behind its hedge. And, above all, then he must know when not to wait any longer. He must know something neither Nietzsche nor Sartre, nor even Heidegger, knows: longing. But before the longing comes the twilight, and then the night. He who is on the mountain will see the sun before those in the valley. Climb then if you dare; the night may not last much longer.

Are we really to assume that the Sunday of history is coming to an end, that day devoted to waiting around instead of worship? One whose Sunday was inhumanly closed by the Nazis, Benjamin Fondane, assures us still that "It is the idea, the obsession, the strange voice of the 'great Monday' which makes the Sunday of history so sombre, so anxious, so long, so impatient." It is easier to believe only half of Kafka's mind, that Sunday will never end; it is hard to believe, without the encouragement of some experience of presence, that we are being reserved for a Great Monday. Can this be made easier by saying that we may have the right to believe and hope for another order, and yet this one may not end?

What of the night, between twilight and dawn, the evening land? How do those who wait in it occupy themselves? Perhaps once, in Greece or Italy, there were "powerful goals and interests capable of absorbing our dreams", as de Rougemont has said. Certainly we have less effulgence, less individual violence, less bright passion, less art. But we are as busy and as productive in our own transient ways. We do not work because we love the work so much as because we want and need recognition. In a world where anonymity is close to everyone, recognition of any sort restores personality and confidence. Men have to be known by others so that they can be sure they know themselves; there are no objective means to evaluate what one is and what one does. Living has become so subjective, that one must appeal to other subjects for a guarantee of one's own position. Those who claim to live off the hump of their own subjectivity—like Sartre—are the ones who have gained the recognition from others that actually discounts their claim. They are the last to submit to the voice of the Great Monday which Heidegger believes he hears resounding beyond the horizon. Let us not be frightened. Out of the silence that surrounds us, we shall hear for the first time the voice of Being. Out of "one of the essential theatres of speechlessness", the dread of the chaos within and outside man to-day, will come the sense of "the pure other than what is . . . nothing, the veil of Being". We must submit to the night so that we may submit to the nothingness that veils Being. How much more seductive is Being for its veil, God for His voice. And how much more credible? Or is Heidegger's mind too devious?

Heidegger understands the nihilism of the twentieth century, but is not a nihilist; he understands the denial or absence of God, and is not an atheist or agnostic. What is he then? "I do not deny God. I state his absence. My philosophy is a waiting for God. Here is the problem of our world. Not in gloom." But the world is in gloom, even if our problem is waiting. If waiting is not denying or expecting, if it is not longing or refusing, what is it? Does one not usually wait for someone one expects? Here is a new kind of waiting, a waiting without longing. We are being reserved for a Great Monday, yet we are not sure we want Monday. If we were sure, we should be longing for it, and longing is beyond our right. We have no right either to expect or to long, and yet we are to wait, according to Heidegger, because we believe there is a Great Monday reserved for someone some time. How can we reconcile this belief with the knowledge of God's continued absence? Heidegger has found an ingenious way of not having his cake and not eating it without denying that there is a cake. We wait for God to speak so that we can name him. Why not name him so that he will speak? Because he might speak? "The holy does indeed appear. But the God remains far off. The time of the reserved discovery is the age when the God is lacking." Is there a difference between the holy and the God? And what does one discover in the age when the God is lacking?—Not God certainly. Is the holy the voice of God, the reverberation over the mountain peaks beyond the castle? Heidegger does not hold men guilty of abandoning God; worse, of abandoning the awareness that God has abandoned them. In this is his superiority. This is the superior knowledge he has that parallels Nietzsche's joyful wisdom that God has died. Of what use is either?

Only the poet or the contemplative philosopher can still hear the sound of the retreating God. The question is: is he retreating further or is he coming our way again? What part we play now depends on the answer we give to this question. Surely Heidegger must think that God is still withdrawn if not retreating. Or does he think that by waiting we encourage God to return? Is waiting meritorious? Those who wait feel, above all, God's absence. If they could only deny his existence and live again in the halcyon twilight of Nietzsche, if not in the Italy of the Renaissance, they could create rather than wait. Then artists would displace contemplatives, and man would once more surpass himself and his history! How little Heidegger is attracted to this vista, how sure he is that even if God is absent his voice can be heard if one listens carefully. No vista can displace this hearing. But to wait unheroically, with neither hope nor expectation, without longing or the right to long, is this not a kind of heroism? Or is it a failure of nerve?

Heidegger says that Heracleitus's famous "ἦθος ἀνθρώπῳ δαίμων" means that man's character is where he lives, that man is at home only in the neighbourhood of God. And he goes on to remind his readers of Aristotle's anecdote about Heracleitus who, when found by the kitchen oven warming himself, said: "There are gods here too." If the gods are near, here, in the kitchen, anywhere, men are not good hosts. And by this time the gods may have left the kitchen for more hospitable environs. Man has not learned to live as a being groping with feelers here and there for traces of divinity. Only when he has understood himself as a being who transcends himself while looking for the Transcendent, will man be able to call himself a being for God as well as a creature of distance. Heidegger has obstinately, and without discussion, assumed that other men are as cut off from Being as he is, and he has tried to justify his own forlornness by calling all others forlorn. But if the others admit even privately that they too are forlorn, then his remarks about God's absence and the waiting for God should force them to ask whether they know something he does not know that can relieve this forlornness, without illusion.

Without relieving himself of this forlornness, he has admitted that "after man has placed himself in the presence of something perpetual, then only can he expose himself to the changeable". And he does not expose himself any more than he can help to the changeable, because he is still waiting for the presence of something perpetual. He understands his own situation, and through his own his contemporaries', as one of homelessness. Man works and waits at a distance from Being, from home "where man endures". The thinker and the poet—he uses Hölderlin and Rilke as his models of the latter—try to come into the presence of Being, or, as he likes to put it, into the neighbourhood or proximity of Being. "The thinker utters Being. The poet names what is holy." Like Max Picard, Heidegger says that only the thinker and the poet care for the words they use to tell of what they hear in the silence in which the "voice of Being" speaks. "Obedient to the voice of Being, thought seeks the Word through which the truth of Being may be expressed." The thinker, more than other men, is a "shepherd of Being". But it should be remarked, parenthetically, that man's guardianship of the truth of Being can bring a sacrifice of his will, his calculation, and his solitude. And yet, as man tells the truth, he thanks reality. For real thinking is a thanking, an act of piety towards what gives and what is given. If the vocation of the thinker is to be shepherd of Being, "the vocation of the poet is a homecoming by which the homeland is first made ready as the land of proximity to the source." The poet prepares the way the thinker is to follow.

Heidegger makes much of Hölderlin's poem, *Homecoming*, for he thinks he sees in it a return not to the source but "to the proximity of origin". Home is where we are nearest our source, but it is not itself the source, "the most Joyous". And such a return is only possible for one who has previously, and perhaps for a long time now, borne on his shoulders as the wanderer the burden of the voyage and has gone over into the source. The essence of proximity seems to consist in keeping near the Near, while keeping it at a distance. Does he not say that "proximity to the source is a mystery"? The nearer we get to grasping the heart of something, the sense of reality, the more ineffable what we see or feel. This is not moral mystery; it is rather noetic, metaphysical. It is quite different from Marcel's conception of at-homeness as a moral readiness, an attentiveness to others. Heidegger, who has been separated by a century of German philosophy and German isolation from the world of moral attentiveness, returns to it so far only as the source of the Joy that will bring the dawn, rather than the sun that will require one who has seen the Good to go back down the mountain into the world. One can understand this difference also as that between a man, like Marcel, who has already left the presence of the sun, and a man, like Heidegger, who is only now approaching it and does not know all that will be required of him. No wonder he thinks that "it is in writing that the principal return home consists". Marcel would have to add to this, "only at first". And we cannot believe, as Proust and Joyce did also, that only the artist can return home. There is a lesson to be learned in this comparison which is more than the comparison of two philosophers, a lesson for those who are just coming out of some isolation. Their first glimpse of home will not be a moral one, but one of selfish joy. But they can know that that joy is only the beginning of a new life.

The Nietzschean joy is experienced again by Heidegger who more specifically understands joy to be "the process of becoming at home in proximity to the source". Is it not pathetic that there must be some fear as well as humbleness—the components of awe—in Heidegger's insistence that man is capable only of being at home in the proximity? Let him not come too close? Let him rejoice only at the end of the night? "We never get to know a mystery by unveiling or analysing it; we only get to know it by guarding the mystery as mystery." But who is he to say what is mystery and what is not? May it not be unveiled and still be mysterious? It is a mystery in which man loses his recent homelessness. It is Being, and also truth. But it is not particular truth, of German guilt, of one's own stupidity or treachery, one's own smallness. It is the overwhelming truth that requires a submission that should leave no room in future for false wandering. So if one asks: "Has Heidegger learned anything?" one might have to reply: "Perhaps not." He has learned no more than any other contemplative before him, but no less either. He is learning of the source of truth, which is greater than man's supposing and wandering, and he is learning as he approaches. It is as if, while he approaches, a philosopher like Marcel departs. For Heidegger the thorn hedge has thinned, and in the hour before dawn the darkness has become less, so that for once and at long last he has been able to catch the presence of the many-hued castle within. For this he has been prepared by his understanding of the absence of "the whole", an absence grievously felt in care, in boredom, in dread. Now, with hedge disarmed, he can feel the beginning of that joy that signifies that he is "within the whole". Whatever one loves makes one aware of the whole. But Heidegger does not yet love, nor is he really joyous, for he still senses the whole by its absence rather than by its proximity.

Heidegger's anatomy of waiting is more significant than one at first supposes, because it is a waiting for presence, not just a waiting. He lives in the presence of (as Marcel would say), in the proximity of, "God's self-withholding". Neither Hölderlin nor himself has "named" God to his face—it will be a new name anyway—for he is not yet distinct from all the names of his creatures, as Being should be distinct from beings, even by name. If we could name Him, Heidegger thinks, then He might appear. But how can He be named unless we have seen Him appear? So near Heidegger comes to Augustine's question: "And how shall they believe without a preacher?" Here Heidegger betrays his bondage to Nietzsche. He cannot believe in a preacher, for he cannot believe anyone has ever before understood what he searches for. And "the God remains afar." If he is right, one might still tell him that he is right partly because there is no God, far or near. If he is right, and God is really afar, we should imitate his contemplative waiting. But suppose he is not right, suppose Augustine is right instead, and the God is here all the time? Then it is man's purging of self and pride that alone will open the eyes. So Dostoyevsky too thought. If God's presence is withheld, are we to feel lucky if we are in the presence of his self-withholding, in proximity to his absence? What does this mean? Does God withhold himself or does man? Is this just another example of German deviousness in hiding its own failures? No doubt waiting is a numb business; is it dumb also? Can absence be felt as well as presence, or only because it envelops presence, like the thorn hedge the castle? Is it not at least possible that many are not aware of the thorn hedge, who live in the valley under the mists that hide both castle and hedge? Is Heidegger bringing in longing by the back-door? Is the character of his waiting, in which absence testifies to presence, so different from the nostalgia which constantly reminds, through the pang of what is lost, what might be found?

And when was anyone able to name God differently? Was there a time for revealed presence? Was it once as easy as attending the feast given by the king and queen for the birth of their daughter? If the many lose touch with presence and fidelity, but either think they are still in touch or care not that they have lost touch, must the exceptionally sensitive and needy lose touch too? And would one be far wrong in wondering whether Heidegger's waiting and Nietzsche's egotism both express the guilt and the insufficiency of Evening-Land at the end of the nineteenth century? And is Heidegger right in supposing that God has only slept and is now near awakening?

Certain it is that he has not defined our time hopefully. And yet he has encouraged men to get near the neighbourhood of God, to walk in the presence of the source of Joy, the Holy, Being. Does presence mean union? And does union mean anything more than not being two, forgetting twoness, absence, separation, isolation? Even if men do not cease to be many, they can live as if one. In space people are separated, but presence is not spatial. When one is in the presence of somebody else, space is irrelevant. This is why presence or "here-ness" seems spatial sometimes, just because it is irrelevant. That is, if it seems spatial, it is because it is, above all, not temporal. Presence—the present (gift)—defies change, unless one is an Indian giver. The presence of someone "fills the room". We feel as if there were "nothing between us". This is union, at-oneness, at-homeness. The nothing in between is what Buber means by his own mysterious "between" in dialogue. It is the feeling we have when we are with someone we are seeing again, or for the first time, the feeling that his being flows out to meet us, charming and enchanting the air we both breathe, the light between us, even the chairs, rugs, curtains, in the room. What meets us, touches us without hands, is so superior to all we ordinarily think of as real that, like Buber, we might attribute such extraordinary awareness to the existence of a "between" which is separable from us. And yet there is nothing in between where all things are made present by apprehension. This is the fact about presence that accounts for both dread and love: there is nothing in between when two are present to each other. But for Heidegger, the shepherd of being, there still is something in between him and the God whose Word he waits to hear out on the mountain, the God whom he cannot yet name. To those who listen to the story of The Sleeping Beauty, there is both instruction and hope in the report that he waits at the end of the night instead of in the twilight, where he met Nietzsche.

3—BEFORE DAWN AND DAWN

"After long, long years, a King's son came again to that country,
  and heard an old man talking about the thorn-hedge,
    and that a castle was said to stand behind it
      in which a wonderfully beautiful princess named Briar-rose
      had been asleep for a hundred years,
    and that the King and Queen and the whole court were asleep
                              [likewise.
He had heard, too, from his grandfather,
    that many Kings' sons had already come,
    and had tried to get through the thorny hedge,
    but they had remained sticking fast in it,
    and had died a pitiful death.
Then the youth said,
        I am not afraid,
        I will go and see the beautiful Briar-rose.
The good old man might dissuade him as he would,
he did not listen to his words."

At first, when the hedge was new and the memory of the castle
still fresh, many noble young men assaulted the hedge and were
caught. So many deaths could not but quiet the passions of
those who had known them, and for many years no one thought
of risking his life. So when another king's son came along,
almost a hundred years later, those who had memory only of
the deaths of his predecessors, must have said: "The fool!" The
more intelligent of them who knew the legend had always
been waiting for this day, but they had expected that the day
would come for those who waited rather than for a man from
another country. A time for waiting is a long time, and those
who wait do not necessarily feel there is time for longing too.
They may half expect without daring to long. One can wait
without longing. The man who waits has learned that acting
may be dangerous. He may even believe that he is waiting for
the fullness of time. One who believes this much is but a short
step from believing in the right to long. But the step may be

impossible for him to take, and he may wait until someone unknown strides past him.

Into this world of sitters near the scent of presence came a king's son, a foreigner. At least he was not known to those who waited as a king's son. Perhaps he had been among them in disguise. He had heard the old man talking about a castle which he himself may never have seen, but which he could almost believe in as one almost believes in a fairy-story. But the king's son did believe, and as it happened it was the right time to believe. And this is why he was the true prince. He knew his vocation, but it was his vocation only because he knew it at the right time. Only then was it appropriate for someone to say, as he said: "I am not afraid, I will go and see the beautiful Briar-rose." For the true prince there are no hedges and no early death, only roses and a Briar-rose.

In our philosophers' mythology Heidegger resembles the canny old man who knows the legend but does not believe in it enough to seize the time. In the same mythology Sartre, the true successor of Nietzsche in the present century, continues the nineteenth-century confidence in assault regardless of the time. Two things mark the character of Sartre and Nietzsche: a denial of God and a complacent assertion of the imprisonment of the self. Sartre, like Nietzsche, holds that love imprisons the self even further, for love prevents the self from exercising its prerogatives wherever it pleases. Like Nietzsche, Sartre cares only for the self's own freedom of choosing and making. There is nothing esoteric about this self-enclosed freedom; it is probably more characteristic of the modern world than any other conception. Sartre himself could simply be echoing Proust who said: "Man is the creature that cannot emerge from himself, that knows his fellows only in himself, and when he asserts the contrary he is lying," or, as Sartre would put it, is in bad faith. Not for Sartre or Proust the more esoteric notion of Heidegger that man is a creature of distance, who travels from himself so that he may meet Being and other beings. Sartre has much to say about transcendence but he does not mean by it that man can ever "emerge from himself". That is why both he and Nietzsche couple the denial of God, a real Transcendent, with the enclosure of the self. And that is why Dostoyevsky, believing in a real Transcendent who is near man, always said that only the man who believes in God will be able to love individual men, although he may love humanity. One kind of transcendent prepares for another; one kind of presence prepares for another. The consequences of a consistent atheism are what Proust had already laid down before Sartre, who in every respect always imitates his predecessors without giving them credit: "The bonds that unite another person to ourselves exist only in our mind. Memory as it grows fainter relaxes them, and notwithstanding the illusion by which we would fain be cheated and with which, out of friendship, politeness, deference, duty, we cheat other people, we exist alone."

For the man who exists, as did Proust, between the period of assault and the period of waiting, between twilight and before dawn, men exist in lone units. And yet even he, with Sartre, admits that there are traces in man of a disposition to emerge, to transcend in a radical, complete way. Proust, living in the night, is not sure of his own pessimism because through his nostalgia he has too strong a sense of presence. His elegy on the death of Bergotte discloses his own inconsistency. Sartre, on the other hand, with no nostalgic sense or experience of presence to haunt him, does not depart from his opinion that man is "a useless passion". Heidegger, living in the pre-dawn of presence, half-believes in a divine order or order of Being that man can wait for. He is close to the Kafka of *The Castle* in his belief in the existence of an order transcending subjectivity —although he rejects the old notion that subjectivity must be transcended by way of an impassable gap between man and

God. He makes no effort, like the surveyor in Kafka's novel, to get in touch with and be recognized by the castle, but waits for the castle to get in touch with him. Nor is he willing, for any reason, to think of recognition by men as a sign or a substitute for such superior recognition.

But man will not be recognized until he himself recognizes. If it is certain that neither Nietzsche nor Sartre has any fondness for particular things or persons except as they confirm their own importance, it is equally clear that until recently Heidegger has shown no attentiveness to persons or nature either, except as illustrations of phenomenological principles. Through his studies of Hölderlin's poetry he has gradually entered into a more emotional relationship with nature, with homeland, and, dimly, with persons. He has never had to overcome Nietzsche's defiance of affection, or Sartre's nausea before material things. But he does not have, even now, the deep and detailed nostalgia for all his experience that so characterizes Proust's novels. And this is why Proust's writing is so much nearer, so much more real than that of the philosophers, not because it is not philosophy but because Proust loved what he was writing about. And, most important of all, Proust did not write only of himself, his freedom, his vision, his denials, his refusals, his hates and defiance. He wrote of a past time, of other people, of places, of manners, of morals, of longings and fulfilments, of expectations and promises, and of non-recognition and loss.

A man can wait without longing, like Heidegger; he can long without expecting, like Proust. But unless he does one or the other, he is "condemned to his freedom", Sartre's and Nietzsche's freedom. The princes who died in the thorn hedge were not true, nor were they really free. And yet they were not materialists either. They had a dim sense of spirit which they called freedom, and they opposed the materialism of their contemporaries, and the crasser kinds of slavery. But the slavery to materialism is only one kind of slavery; another is the slavery to a conception of spirit which does not admit presence. These free spirits wanted to be recognized so that they could live, and yet they had no prior experience of recognition which could tell them that true recognition is of presence rather than spirit. For spirit, like presence of mind, can be a camouflage for an inability to be present without show and motion. Presence is not always marked by spiritedness. Where there is spiritedness and no giving, there is only deception, no presence. And such deception covers only lightly an uneasiness that presence alone can still.

There are persons who suffer what Elizabeth Bowen has called "death of the heart". Or, is it more correct to say that there may be some persons who cannot suffer "death of the heart"? The heart which can die from squeezing—for the heart wants to love and be loved—can recover from early rebuffs only because it longs to get in touch with the presence that can fulfil it. But there comes a time when deceit and indifference may shock the heart into numbness, when life permits a squeezing until hope and affection are tight and dry. At this time solitude enters with its dark face, and is ensconced until comfort is assured by the presence of some sane being. Without a new presence or a new awareness of an old presence, the heart can be squeezed dead. How many failures of nerve express this kind of bereftness? Only those who can see in their ordeals opportunities to enter an order which they do not yet live openly in, will have the courage to hope for an end to solitude, and a resumption on another level of awareness, of life's ideals.

It is easy enough to define the conditions of hope when one's situation is not in danger. But we should be intelligent enough to see that some people have every right to be convinced that, "If there is a paradise, it is not for me." This is another way of saying with Nietzsche: "If there are Gods, they do not care for us." It is a scepticism tinged with regret, that is born of bad luck. It is the underside of the apparently frivolous position which, as in the following snatch of conversation, shows a disbelief in paradise accompanied by some sense that paradise somehow can be encountered.

> " 'I was brought up to be honest; the trouble is it gets me nowhere.'
> Liking her better, he smiled and said: 'It'll get us to heaven.'
> 'Will it?'
> 'If heaven existed.'
> 'Do you not believe in heaven, Mr. Fielding, may I ask?' she said,
> looking at him shyly.
> 'I do not. Yet I believe that honesty gets us there.' "
>
> *(Passage to India).*

Mr. Forster does not believe in heaven, and yet he believes honesty will take us wherever we are going. He cannot—and is it possible to say because he has not suffered as severely as some?—let himself be convinced by those who feel we are going nowhere. His attitude has this in common with the saying, "If there is a paradise, it is not for me": the touchstone is not whether one be rational or irrational, but whichever part of one's life one can stress. When all goes well, honesty looms big; when things turn out badly, who does not feel excluded from paradise? The point of the comparison, however, does not lie in this distinction but in the fact that both statements refer to another order of things to which man is probably not related. There is a recognition in both, that there is some sense in speaking of paradise, even metaphorically.

Even Proust—or should one really say especially Proust?—who was so convinced by experience that man cannot emerge from himself, wondered whether a man mourning the death of a friend might not want to believe in paradise. His fictional counterpart does wonder, after the death of the writer Bergotte: "He was dead. Permanently dead? Who shall say? All we can say is that everything is arranged in this life as though we entered it carrying the burden of obligations contracted in a former life. There is no reason inherent in the conditions of life on this earth that can make us consider ourselves obliged to do good, to be fastidious, to be polite. All these obligations which have not their sanction in our present life seem to belong to a different world, founded upon kindness, scrupulosity, self-sacrifice, a world entirely different from this, which we leave in order to be born into this world, before perhaps returning to the other to live once again beneath the sway of those unknown laws which we have obeyed because we bore their precepts in our hearts, knowing not whose hand had traced them there—those laws to which every profound work of the intellect brings us nearer and which are invisible only— and still—to fools." What more powerful argument for another order is there? This is Platonic in import, if not wholly in conviction. Proust was no more certain than Forster is, that there is a paradise, but he felt that if there was one, we should return to it precisely by means of our sense of moral obligation— in Gabriel Marcel's language, our sense of presence—which could be called a symptom of a supernatural order. The difference between Proust and Forster—as far as these texts go—is that Proust lacks Forster's detachment from death and suffering. And although, unlike Forster, he tries to belittle his instinctive pity and yearning, he has to admit that his moral instincts may be indicative of a transcendent moral order. This is far from the saying: "Man is a creature who cannot emerge from himself." It is nearer the cry of Chekhov in *The Three Sisters*: "Oh, just a little more and we shall know what it is all about!" And Chekhov had, in saying this, already applied for admittance to the house of longing, even if he was never to live there. What is so interesting about Chekhov's permanent undercurrent of longing and regret is that through it one feels as if there were but a veil separating a man from the truth that saves, the life that charms for ever, just another breath, one more word, another try, one more chance. The fact that the word or effort or chance never comes, does not discredit the longing, not completely at any rate. The truth, "la vraie vie" (Proust), the life that enchants us, may be here anyway, in spite of our blindness or our bad luck. In Chekhov we live sentimentally, watching illusions and disillusions, conspiring with a land in which longing is not only allowed but seated as on a seesaw.

When we read Chekhov, we wonder whether the laws of probability—are there any?—must continue to work against the heart's longing. And while we admit that Chekhov seems to say: "Yes, always!" we still want to know whether he authorizes despair. May we guess that the laws of probability are not to be measured only by disillusion but sometimes by the longing that arises from certain crucial personal experiences? Would mankind continually cling to longing if there were not an order of things in which longing sometimes comes to rest? And comes to rest, not in an unseen world, but here and now? This kind of argument cannot be fully persuasive, of course. It cannot persuade anyone who does not know from experience the connection between longing and the fulfilment in moments of presence. We do know that most other dispositions within the soul relate to some natural order. Moments of presence are natural too, within experience, and in some sense verifiable. And there seems to be some connection between these moments and the longing for a less verifiable order of which these moments may be the outposts. Or they may not. But this is the kind of thing Tolstoy had in mind when he made Prince Andrew reply to Pierre's arguments on behalf of a kingdom of truth: "What convinces us when we see a being dear to us, bound up with our own life . . . and suddenly that being is seized with pain, suffers, and ceases to exist. . . . Why? It cannot be that there is no answer. And I believe there is . . . All I say is that it is not argument that convinces me of the necessity of of a future life, but this: when you go hand in hand with someone and all at once that person vanishes there, into nowhere, and you yourself are left facing that abyss, and look in. And I have looked in." One order suggests—it does not prove—another. And, oddly, for some it is the order of hardest disillusion which suggests the order aimed at by longing; loss suggests presence. An experience of this sort, the loss of a wife or a child, can dissolve the paralysis of suspended belief— waiting—and suggest a land where there is no loss.

My third example of the suggestiveness of longing is taken from Turgenev's *On the Eve*, where his heroine Elena asks: "Why must we die, why must we suffer separation's illness and tears? And if we must, then why all this beauty, why this sweet feeling of hope, why this reassuring sense of some immortal guardianship? What then is the meaning of that smiling, beneficent sky, of this earth so happy at its ease? Can all this be only what we feel within us—whereas outside, in reality, there is only an eternal icy stillness? Can it be that we are quite alone? Then why this thirst for prayer, why does prayer give us joy?" There are three questions in this passage. Why must we die, why illness and separation? If we die, why beauty? And why hope and prayer? Is there any answer man can honestly give to the first? We can only seek consolation. But the second question can be answered variously, by way of Plato or Proust, for example. We come into this world bearing the traces of another world. This is that lost paradise of Proust, the world or the ideas of Plato. The third question would not be understood by Proust, who did not thirst for either prayer or joy. Its atmosphere is unashamed longing. You cannot long until you have gone past the recognition of the possibility of longing— so far Proust could go—to the practice of prayerful longing. The world of longing is religious, in the fullest sense, and unless longing is complemented by praying, it is unstable and can be dissolved by disillusionment. When a man prays, he has already passed beyond the period of waiting. And if longing is religious, it is also true that the man who knows how to long knows also how to be loyal. The reason is that he has

93

an appreciation of stability. The true prince is true to his vision, to his word, and to those who trust him. His longing, like his loyalty, aims at some other than self. The very occasion for his longing may well be the occasion for his bearing testimony of his loyalty to someone apparently lost, through death, or illness, or separation. Through longing, the land of personal loyalties—of promises and their fulfilments—begins to come to life.

This coming to life through the suggestiveness of longing, of the world of moral and psychological fulfilment, is what one has in mind when one thinks of life as a return. No one wants to return to the banalities or failures of the past, but to the fulfilments that one once understood but did not experience, in longing for them. One sees around one many times in life occasions and realities to be held tight in complete delight, and one leaves them knowing one has not had time to do so. The time arrives only later, when one returns in memory or nostalgia with more time, and with more understanding. One returns to the stability and loveliness in the persons and places, to whom one can be more loyal in returning this way than ever in their presence. Or so it sometimes seems. How much of life can be fairly thought of in terms of a turning-back, a recurrence? Do we want to turn back only when we meet obstacles? Or do obstacles sometimes provide occasions not only for reassessment but for revivification? To turn back permits us to recognize something permanent and independent, which endures without us but without which we can barely endure. In days of heady crisis for civilizations as well as for individuals, when men feel cut off from a future that has promised adventure and advancement, they can survive, at least for a time, as long as they have a past to return to. If this is denied them, or—what amounts to the same—if the truth about the past is denied them, they will cease to appreciate the connection between their freedom and their stability. It is

94

what one freely longs for and is given, not what one has to accept, that completes humanity. Men lose their sense of the independence of history when they keep windows to the past open only by habit or by propaganda, instead of by study and wonderment. They do not understand that the journey to the past is only a detour to the future, prescribed for human voyagers because man does not carry all his absolutes within him. Man is always mending his roads, tearing up stretches he has worn through, using the back roads as substitutes until he can lay down new road beds. Tyrants understand that this is the process of freedom which obstructs the achievement of simplified solutions. They know that they can control men most completely when they control their memories. The only return they let men envisage—and they permit this natural tendency to function so far—is a return to a mythical past which their propagandized present or future imitates. Where the tyrant lets man's tendency to return to a vision of stability function through myth, the bourgeois lets the same tendency function through repetition. The bourgeois likes to go back to the same place, see the same people at certain times and in certain places, over and over. He revels in his routines or banalities because for him they are stable. But their stability is unexplored, if not unexplorable; they are reassuring but not revivifying. In fact, he lacks even the primitive imagination of the tyrant who embellishes his simplicities with a glorious if mythical past. The Tyrant appeals to something in people who have had enough of repetition, repetition of routines as well as poverty.

How different from these two extremes of mimicking a return, is Proust's return to a real, not far distant past which he gets to know more exactly only as he returns to it in memory and nostalgia. It is, unlike the other examples, inexhaustibly rich in sentiment and fact. There is no end to it, even if it was all contained within a few years of one man's life and field of vision. There is no end to it as there is no end to "a breath of fresh air", which is the sign of nostalgic as opposed to contrived memory. There is something of the infinite in a breath of fresh air, in the new married to the familiar. But how strange this would sound to people who for years had been played on, blown through so that they sounded like steam organs. The air is fresh because it is refreshed; the vision is lovely because it contains the loveliness we had but never knew, we knew of but never had. Joy is the new that is at the same time the most familiar. The sudden presence, the arrival back where one started, is refreshing just because we have breathed it once before—"of that purer air which the poets have vainly tried to establish in Paradise, whereas it could not convey that profound sensation of renewal if it had not already been breathed, for the only true paradise is always the paradise we have lost". Proust would not have us think that there is no paradise to enter, but only that we may have already known it and become estranged from it. How close this is to Dostoyevsky's fervent belief that "paradise is here if only we knew it". We reach paradise again by way of a journey from paradise, a paradise whose loss we mourn. But the bitterness of loss is mixed with the ecstasy of approaching return. The past, the lost paradise, re-presented as a "permanent essence" is our vision of "the one true paradise".

This view of life as a return makes of life a more unified affair than either the tyrant or the bourgeois would guess. But life is unified through the detour to presence by a sensitivity which is hard to maintain in a world which requires bustle and noise. That is why human nature as a last resort for its health has arranged to remind the soul of presence through the spontaneous eruption of the unconscious mind. This is nostalgia's role in our time, the symptom of a last resort. What the conscious mind cannot bear to or is not trained to or is not allowed to experience, the unconscious conscience brings forth at embarrassing moments. "Here," it says, "is what you loved and lost; compare it to this false moment!" Such is the effect of the care of the historian or the novelist, that, similarly, we say: "Here is what we should have known." No one wants paradise because it is lost, because it is past. No one wants the past. It is the present and its presences that we want, and we need the past only to bring us to its presence which we extract from time and change. No one wants the future either, because it has not come yet and therefore has no value; no one wants the future just because it is ahead. One can want it to get away from the present, but not from presence, if we have it. It is the presence *in* the future, on the model of the presence *in* the past, the presence which this moment does not seem to give us, presence wherever it is that longing aims for. We want only that freshness that is ever familiar, that familiarity that is ever new. And so men long, if they dare, only because they have been reminded either by nostalgia or by some experience of presence, either artificial, as in literature and history, or actual, as in personal encounters.

In the fullness of time the true prince arrives. Then the new day and its new order dawn. But much has to pass before night ends. We roll and toss before we sleep, dreaming of those triumphs which are so implausible in the day. We may have to lie waiting in watchful numbness until we are called or until some alarm goes off—and then perhaps only to find that others are up before us. There are always a few chosen ones who wake in the small hours, because a child has cried, or to relieve nature, and before they can sleep again they are visited by the most desolating temptation, the temptation to believe that they have failed. For them the new day cannot bring hope or change. But their hour of collapse is also the time of longing. Only in their most anguished hour does longing burn so fiercely, promising to consume even the anguish. In the early hours of the morning, when free spirits, and those who wait, sleep on, the true prince awakes of his own accord and is tempted to give up. Will his longing exceed his anguish? His test of strength has come, and the fibres of his character tremble from the battle between disbelief and resolution. If longing triumphs, he can set out "searching for something more mysterious. It is the path told of in books, the ancient, obstructed path to which the weary prince could find no entrance. It is found at last at the most forlorn hour of the morning." (Alain-Fournier.) But make no mistake, the prince did not find the entrance at once. He had to reconnoitre the thorn hedge a long time before some sign from the sky or from the sleeping flowers in the briars told him that day was not far off.

Through the night man's restlessness gathers, until the pressure is too strong and awakens those beside the hedge whose waiting is their sleeping. Not everyone wakes by himself, and not everyone listens in that pre-dawn silence, that silence which "makes men long for that condition before the Fall". (Picard.) In this silence a man feels his sickness for home or love struggling against its suppression. Which will win, the fear of loss or the nearness of the loved presence? Sometimes a man has to become homesick in order to know his home, lovesick to know his love. Both home and love may ask of the individual more than he can give. Neither home nor love will settle for a loan. We cannot give them only half of our attention. They haunt us, thrusting their fear, aching, warning fear, on us. They remind us of the day just past without home or love, a past of days misspent. So runs the course of longing, haunting, in the pre-dawn quiet, when alone in the house we stay awake and have to decide before sunrise whether to welcome or stifle the longing. The true prince, no doubt, does welcome this positive conscience and goes forward even before sunrise to reconnoitre. There is only one true prince.

Longing has its time, its occasion, and its appointment. They go together. He who longs does not exceed the occasion; if he did, he would cease to long, he would simply be assuming that there could be no question of his right. But the true prince is confident because he has received his appointment and knows he has not fully earned it. Who is there, he says, who fully earns all he is given? The gods' gifts to men are greater than men's deserving. How could it be otherwise? The true prince does not presume beyond the terms of his appointment; he has a charge which belongs to him only because he has been more attentive than other men. He has stretched his hearing and stretched his heart until it longs across the abyss surrounding mortal man, to the order whose voice men await in trepidation. Will the voice speak? Will one be chosen? And the answer seems to be: "Not unless someone wants very much."

Is this Being worth the heartache, the long anxiety of the fretful night, worth the difficult patience before success held off? Is it worth the knightly vigil before an altar that may have no presence, only bread? Is the voice there? Is it approaching? Is it here among us? Will it snort or bless? Or, in the silence, will there be more silence? Will all else be lost with disillusion, will all else return compensated? Can there be a real audition? In the pre-dawn anguish the soul is tempted, haunted, tested. Can it pause, breathless, shriven, angered? Can it seize the haunting vision and dedicate itself to its seductive promise? The terms of this promise and appointment are clear only to one who is practised in the many nostalgic returns which men make from year to year. To the unpractised, nostalgia is just a moment of weakness, filled with pleasure as well as pain.

Once upon a time there was a man who wanted to return to a city where he had spent some months as a student. His life was filled by a yearning to return to this place he had not been particularly happy in. The very ordinariness of his longing for this part of the past should convince one that nostalgia does not tell us only of the most obvious losses or adorations. Nostalgia is not a hothouse sentiment of sickly, lazy minds. The man in this story lived a busy, useful life; he had a family. There was nothing wrong with him as these things are ordinarily understood. And yet every so often he would see and feel himself back in that European city. It was a city of many old churches, surrounding walls, little squares with fountains; it had a river and was built on several levels. From it one could see snow-capped mountains; around it were fine country walks. In the daytime he had wandered about the town, and even years later he could remember paths, streets, corners, shops. It was almost as if he had been sent there to get to know the city for an invading army. One day he returned to this city of his nostalgia, not because he had to but because he wanted to find out what would happen to him and his nostalgia. He stayed for a week. He and his wife took walks all over it. The first time they passed something he had wanted to see again, his student days came back with something of the glow of the past. But when he passed a church or a *pension* for the third time, he had ceased to feel it. He wondered what made things matter once but not thrice. And he decided that most things matter to us as long as we are not sure what they have for us. As soon as we have catalogued their value, we tend to lose interest. And we lose interest even faster in places than in persons, for we know that places do not have any reserve of surprise to thrust on us as even relatives have. He concluded that the familiar is a bore unless it is capable of movement. When friends asked him whether this return to the past had cured him of his longing for it, he had to answer: "No." For he had not returned to the presence which nostalgia had given him the sense of, but to the reality which in the present he was still incapable of experiencing as presence, except momentarily.

This is the story of an ordinary nostalgia which was tested out with an ordinary return that failed. The question now is: "Can any longing be assured of more satisfying fulfilment?"

Or must the longing always be more heart-warming, more promising, than the return it begs for? Does one return to anything more than one's own imagination, which is always untouched, except momentarily, by reality? Where is the fullness that can reply definitively to longing? Where is the presence that touches our lives the way nostalgia, sentiment of presence, touches our imagination? Where is the paradise we know we have lost? Where is the loved one whose image haunts? Where is the land we long for that we have never seen,[36] or the century long vanished? Where is presence? Here is longing, but where is the presence longed for? Or is there only longing? Is all longing only a moving, by which we are moved to no satisfying end? Is there an empty restlessness that never gets to know love? Is there a promising that knows no giving in return? Nostalgia gives to the imagination "the idea of existence", as Proust says, that it usually lacks. Is there some existent somewhere, some time, that will give itself "for good" to the whole person?

Love and nostalgia cannot be separated. One does not love that which one has not already known. One is nostalgic for that which one would have return. In both love and nostalgia a wave of presence swirls around with a wave of loss. Which will subside first depends on the intelligence of our belief. We are not nostalgic for mud or evil, for what has hurt us, for suffering. We are not nostalgic for tragedy, or for comedy, or for whatever is unfriendly. We are homesick only for what makes happy sense to us. No one wants to return to disaster, or even to the ridiculous—we can always have either. We might sometimes think we were returning to the ridiculous when we return to a world where laughter is allowed, as in Jane Austen or Trollope. But it is not the mockery of false dignity that we long for, but the true dignity of the past. In nostalgia the feeling of creativity, of the future with new presences, of the presences that are coming near us, should succeed the sense of loss. There is an intelligent and un-intelligent way of handling nostalgia, a way of sickening under it and a way of using it. We are likely to be self-enclosed, too conscious of consciousness to get across the fences of our egoism even by means of nostalgia which hits us hard. We need understanding of its role to support any resolution to use it as a means to an end we need.

Some people think that nostalgia is a confession of failure, that the successful man need never be nostalgic. In a world where everything that a man does, wants, or values can be reduced to success or failure, that would be a plausible opinion. We are, however, not that simple. No success can exclude all longing, all regret and restlessness. Longing tells us not only of what we have missed but of what we still need to make it come true. Hearts ache not for success, which we may already have, but for "real presence" which success does not know. How are we to understand else "this desire for our own far-off country . . . the scent of a flower we have not found, the echo of a time we have not heard, news from a country we have never yet visited"? (C. S. Lewis.)[37] Mr. Lewis's answer supports our contention. "Our lifetime nostalgia, our longing to be reunited with something in the universe from which we now feel cut off, to be on the inside of some door which we have always seen from the outside, is no mere romantic fancy, but the truest index of our real situation." Our real situation is needy beyond the solution of sheer energy and success. We need real presences, not only nostalgic ones; we think we find them in loving, in nature, in the Eucharist, in art.

We seek these presences in their own lands wherever they may be; in the "Landes" of Mauriac, that "sad and secret land" in France, where one of his heroines longed to go back to, "there to set forth on the great adventure of the human soul, the search for God"; in Hardy's Wessex or on Aksakoff's steppes; or on the Yorkshire moors of the Brontë sisters. These are places we have not seen save through their representation to us as places others have longed for. We can see the difference between worldly success and presence so clearly, so obviously, in Catherine Earnshaw's violent longing for earth and heath. "I was only going to say that heaven did not seem to be my home; and I broke my heart with weeping to come back to earth; and the angels were so angry that they flung me out in the middle of the heath on the top of Wuthering Heights where I woke sobbing for joy." But the successful man identifies what he grabs with himself; nothing is greater than his power to subdue it. The heath is greater than Catherine Earnshaw; the Wessex countryside more lovely than Tess; the city of our childhood holidays more lovely than our jabber about it. We are charmed by these lands; the successful man is charmed only by himself. The man looking for presence longs for a permanent companion, a god, which will accompany his unending joyous exploration.

"The permanent essence of things" (Proust), the nostalgia of place names and tunes, of scents and sights, we can never wear thin or eat up. They are for us but are not ours. They are with us, but not to be given away at will. Let us not try to control what should guide us. We should not appoint, for we ourselves are given and appointed. We shall not be true to our own idea of ourselves if we are not recognized. Why then are we not recognized more often? Why is it that, as Mr. Lewis has said, "Part of the bitterness which mixes with the sweetness of that message is due to the fact that it so seldom seems to be a message intended for us, but rather something we have overheard?" Is not the answer that what is meant for us is greater than us, independent of us, more unique than we usually are? And should not anything unique, standing by itself, be for all, not only for one who will possess it exclusively? Presence is "something we have overheard", but no less caressing or significant. We may not be sure we were meant to hear or that the voice was speaking to us. But does this timidity matter? Is it not preferable to the assumption that whatever we hear speaks to us only? We have no right—for we are not all true princes—to be sure of our appointment at the rose hedge. We let loose longing without assurance and expectation. We are not sure, completely sure that we are the ones. We meet another order, another land, a world in the words of others. We meet a parallel presence that seduces us but does not necessarily touch us. We may be deluded; there may be a sea mirage. If we are instructed, we are prepared for anything and avoid over-confidence.

Through longing man approaches presence. But longing does not touch and is not touched in return. Longing bears the hurt of loss and failure; it begs for some healing that will last. Longing is the corridor to the land of poetic justice, the justice that is final and real but known only in poetry. It takes intelligence and it takes courage to keep on longing in a world which is organized to refute it. It takes patience to follow longing long enough to stand in the presence of the voices we have overheard in the rose garden. Perhaps they are speaking about us, perhaps even to us, but equally perhaps against us. Perhaps the princess has spoken aloud in her sleep and the time is come for the prince to awaken her.

4—IN THE FULLNESS OF TIME

"But by this time the hundred years had just passed,
  and the day had come when Briar-rose was to awake again.
    When the King's son came near to the thorn hedge,
  it was nothing but large and beautiful flowers,
      which parted from each other of their own accord,
      and let him pass unhurt,
        then closed again behind him like a hedge.

In the castle yard he saw the horses and the spotted hounds lying asleep;
  on the roof sat the pigeons with their heads under their wings.
    And when he entered the house,
  the flies were asleep upon the wall,
  the cook in the kitchen was still holding out his hand to seize the boy,
  and the maid was sitting by the black hen which she was going to

He went on farther,   [pluck.
  and in the great hall he saw the whole of the court lying asleep,
  and up by the throne lay the King and Queen.

Then he went on still farther,
  and all was so quiet that a breath could be heard,
  and at last he came to the tower,
  and opened the door into the little room where Briar-rose was

There she lay,   [sleeping.
    so beautiful that he could not turn his eyes away.
And he stooped down and gave her a kiss.

  But as soon as he kissed her,
Briar-rose opened her eyes and awoke,
  and looked at him quite sweetly.

Then they went down together.

And the King awoke, and the Queen, and the whole court,
  and looked at each other in great astonishment.

And the horses in the courtyard stood up and shook themselves,
  the hounds jumped up and wagged their tails,
  the pigeons upon the roof pulled out their heads from under their
    looked round, and flew into the open country.   [wings,

The flies on the wall crept again,
  the fire in the kitchen burned up and flickered and cooked the meat,
  the roast began to turn and sizzle again,
  and the cook gave the boy such a box on the ear that he screamed,
  and the maid finished plucking the fowl.

And then the marriage of the King's son with Briar-rose
  was celebrated with all splendour,
  and they lived contented to the end of their days."

Can a man know the dividing time between longing and fulfilment? The diurnal recurrence looks the same from one day to another. Every day a new day dawns. Every day there comes the night. Day after day the thorn hedge looked the same in the morning, with the bones of those that died in it still visible. Only one who believes in the direction of his pre-dawn longing can sense anything new in the coming day. Only the true prince may think of ignoring the past and the one hundred years of sleep for the castle and its people. When the fullness of time does come, many will still not believe. And if they begin to believe they may make the mistake of thinking the prince more important than Briar-rose. But the prince has been chosen and called; he remains anonymous to the end. He is not the bringer of tidings, but like a priest he has come to celebrate a sacrament of revivification, to restore a "real presence".

When time was full, the briars turned to flowers. Or is it possible that the briars had always been roses to those who went to touch and not to possess? Could there have been no century of sleep for all, no separation of authority from its subjects, and no real fullness of time? Is any time full when a person looks for presence? Does a fullness of time exclude a deserving? Can a presence be given if it has not been longed for? Can it be longed for if it has not been known? Can it be known if much else is not known? "Who can call on Thee, not knowing Thee?" "Or is it rather that we call on Thee that we may know Thee?" To us the prince is anonymous to the end, but in meeting the princess he loses the anonymity by which he has known himself. He is anonymous to us because we are meant to notice and remember the presence that justified him, and not his deserving. And yet without his deserving the princess would have slept on for us as well.

Who is Briar-rose who sleeps and is awakened? Why is beauty awakened before her father, the king? When an age is obsessed by liberty, which it lacks, it does not seek authority. But it will seek the daughter of authority: order, harmony, loveliness. It may be that if one seeks beauty one is inclined to be indifferent to authority. And yet it seems that authority does not awaken until beauty does. Beauty, like evil, lives by herself, and man must climb the tower to meet her for the first time. All the rest of life awakens after that. The world is transformed by beauty, not by authority or any other virtue. Had not the Wise Women promised all the other virtues as well? They knew the value of their gifts. They did not promise love, for anyone would know that love would follow beauty. And that is why Briar-rose is called Sleeping Beauty, not Sleeping Love. She is called by what she is, not by what man thinks of her. For beauty is objective; it does not depend for its charm or its power on any subjective motive or appraisal. Love may or may not sleep while beauty sleeps, but love cannot but awake when beauty does. Love may be false, may make mistakes; when faced with beauty, man leaves self behind. He enters a world where order and justice are visible, where the reward presents itself to and yet above man's deserving. Only a pure heart can respond by touching what has touched it first. And only a pure heart can afford to forget self long enough to awaken the presence that will give it renown forever.

But the story, as Grimm told it, does not say: "They lived happily forever after." It merely says: "They lived contented to the end of their days." Our days do have an end, however much we keep this from ourselves. And as this is not, at least ostensibly, a story of heaven or of life beyond the grave, what it says has to be taken as it is given, as a journey from the world of probability to a world where truth, beauty, and justice reign. In the fullness of time the true prince has come to awaken the sleeping princess. Their lives have been divided into days of promise and frustration, the years of sleep and longing, and the fulfilment that will have an end. But why must there be an end? Is this just? Is this what was longed for?

Men do not seem to get what they want most, except by accident. It is not always possible to believe that the deserving are rewarded, even if you allow that you may not know the deserving. But what do men want? If they want the things that vanish, does it matter if they miss? If they want what belongs to a land where all things are present, can they fail? What are our numbered days but occasions for preparing to leave the order of failure and probability for an order of presence? We live in a world where restlessness and worse make us disagreeably conscious of loss and what we may lose. We rarely find, we are rarely given, what we do not lose sooner or later. And yet most men do not have the courage to long for the fullness of time—for each man a different time and a different fullness—when he can awaken some sleeping presence. They do not have the courage because they are not encouraged to believe that what they need most is within their reach, if not already experienced. Presence is never lost forever; we merely break contact with it or it breaks contact with us. Presence is not in a world inaccessible to us—a dream world or a supernatural world. Presence is within reach of us all the time, in those we like very much or love, in the seaside and the countryside, in paintings and music, in our ideals of justice. Presence is inextricably mixed with the perishable world which we do not trust, the plausible, clever, manageable world. But presence does not perish with it, nor can presence be manipulated with it. Presence is with it but not of it, and all we have to do is to recognize presence to awaken it. In awakening it we awaken what cannot perish, what will always be loyal to us, what can sleep but never die.

And what does this tell of us? Do not we die even as we

sleep? And are we too not presences? Does not man long for eternity, immortality, the forever after? Can one be satisfied by saying that it is prudent to seek for presence before seeking for eternity? Is it wiser to seek the vertical, momentary vision of what is, before seeking a horizontal, forever, extending life without any vision? Perhaps man is not meant to understand the forever-after until he meets the here-and-now. The land of poetic justice is mysterious enough as we encounter it now and then, but it can be encountered. And we know little enough of what it is we encounter. We may live for eternity and resurrection; we come alive through presence. As longing is the corridor to presence, may not presence be the corridor to eternity? We cannot know what is beyond the end of our days, but we can enter an order of things which can make us say: "I am not afraid." And why should we fear when we have had several chances to awaken the presences we require? If beauty could be awakened even after one hundred years of sleep, if someone could get through the thorn hedge into beauty's presence, what is there to fear? If it is the fullness of time and the true prince which will restore all that seems lost, why be anxious? If we believe in poetry, may we not believe in justice too? The answer is inescapable: "Only if we believe in a poetry which has experienced presence." The poet speaks presence; the philosopher prepares the way. It may be better to be a poet, but it is necessary that man understand what he hears.

We have been exploring so far a phantom land, a fairyland, yet not the least real of all the lands our minds walk in. And we have been exploring it in words, between the poet and the philosopher, away from the poet's silence and the philosopher's argumentativeness. The intimate character of this land, the closest and dearest of all the mind's prairies, makes any mention of it risk sounding either sentimental or abstract. But sometimes it is seen by us as the sea in an island cove on the morning after a hurricane; sometimes it can be seen as

I myself once saw land after being lost in the fog for only half an hour, as the unexpected familiar scene stroking my panic. Man has to approach this land of legend and discovery which we are calling the order of poetic justice, through various ordeals, including the several divisions of tragedy. But even tragedy introduces the hard-hearted and confident only to an ante-room, a waiting-room, before the throne room of justice. Only those who suffer much know what is to be found there, and they may not meet it.

As men try to fulfil through their own efforts their ideals, they become more orderly and ordered by the ordeals they pass through. Their trials mould their values into the shape of an order transcending their pettier desires. As they find their values gradually aligning themselves with an order of things greater than themselves, on the one hand, and smaller than themselves, on the other, they are given the chance of recognizing once for all the goal of their search for stability and delight. Just what this goal is called does not matter; we call it here poetic justice. And we think that in experience first and in philosophical analysis afterwards, this goal of stability and delight which most men strive for consciously, is the same order of charity which the Christian religion speaks of in other words. But to say that presence is charity is to say too quickly that there is a supernatural order which Christian scripture announces and which men pay lip service to without understanding its connection with the rest of their experience. For it is the ideal, if not the answer, that religion and poetry have in common: the ideal of presence. Whether there is a redemptive order which is the same as the revivifying order of moral and psychological presence, is, unfortunately, another question.

Each order of experience has its own atmosphere. The atmosphere of presence, of giving, of wholeness, is silence. We know that serious things have to be done in silence, because we do not have words to measure the immeasurable. In silence men love, pray, listen, compose, paint, write, think, suffer. These experiences are all occasions of giving and receiving, of some encounter with forces that are inexhaustible and independent of us. These are easily distinguishable from our routines and possessiveness as silence is distinct from noise. Whatever is within our control, like fighting or playing, travelling and talking, trading and manufacturing, we do noisily, because we do not have to be respectful before some source of power greater than our meddling. This world where noise breaks loose is a patchwork world where we try to remedy by our own devices the defects of the human condition and human vileness.

The one who best understands the counter world, "the world of silence",[38] is Max Picard. And he tells us that "Once silence lay upon everything, and man had to break through silence in order to think or speak or act." Silence was as objective as anything is now. Now man has to break through noise, of radio, automobiles, and aeroplanes, and crowded dwellings, to hear himself think. Only in sick-room, studies, monasteries, or in the country does one find silence any more. Silence means, for the consciousness, attentiveness; noise means a self-enclosing to protect one from the torrent of calls from the outside. We do not often realize how many separate voices and noises are at one time forcing their messages on us. We cannot notice each for fear of being overwhelmed. So we shut out all but our voices. We say of others that they seldom listen to the other half of a conversation; they wait for their companion's noise to stop so that they can carry on. "Nothing has changed the nature of man so much as the loss of silence," because "the trace of the divine is guarded by silence." Whether this is true or not, it is certain that the trace of presence is guarded by silence. It is no wonder that, in a world, in both West and East now, that manufactures more and more instruments preventing privacy and silence, men are so little persuaded of anything moral or religious that transcends their security or their possessiveness. Picard, who writes as a Christian, says that "The Word has supremacy over silence, but the Word becomes stunted if it has lost connection with silence." So man's sense of presence becomes stunted and snickering if man has lost connection with silence. Picard, like Pascal, thinks of mankind as dispersed, separated, terrifyingly alone, surrounded by a silence in which they could catch the reverberation of God's thunder or God's whisper if they dared to keep still long enough. Like Heidegger, he says that men need language, not as a substitute for God's Word, but as a way of understanding the silence. If we understand men properly, we will have to think of them as solitary offshoots of the divine whisperer, the Silent One, the Deus Absconditus. At best men live in a world of compassion where jabbering is anathema. And all men choose either compassion or jabbering. The more we chatter, the busier we seem, but the farther from God's silence and God's Word. Or, in the language of experience, the farther from the presences that speak to us. The farther we flee from God's presence, the more our faces too show our desperation and disorientation. Picard's three famous books, *The Human Face*, *The Flight from God*, and *The World of Silence*, have all illustrated his central preoccupation with the evidences in modern life of man's cutting himself off from the presence that gives him life. He repeats Kierkegaard's prescription: "If I were a physician and anyone asked me, what would you advise, I would reply: make silence! Bring men to silence. The word of God cannot be heard this way." The world of faith, of prayer, of the sacraments, and of charity is a silent one. But so is the world of serious experience, of most satisfying experience. How much difference is there between these worlds? Is there a difference?

We shall not understand the relevance of mentioning the

divine alongside poetic justice unless we can reduce, in some plausible way, the theological frame of reference to its equivalent in our experience. Is there such an equivalence? Is moral presence equivalent to theological presence? Brunner, a Protestant theologian, has said what Marcel, a Catholic and a philosopher, could agree with: "That which morally is called the lack of charity, might be called metaphysically the fact of not being there for others." We are commonly there, all there, for ourselves; we strive to gain presence of mind. But we usually only pretend to be there for others. We are seldom attentive to others for we do not have enough rest in us to be able to listen to the unrest of someone else. When we are present to them, we act charitably. But we cannot achieve this charitableness merely at will. Charity is a gift; it is the sign of presence (presents). We do not seem to have at beck and call the power to give ourselves completely unless we are giving what we know we ourselves have received. We give well only when something is given to us. We respond rather than assault.

Moments of charity, of being present to someone else, are the exceptions, not the rule. We achieve them only in exceptional situations: as in nostalgia, in love, in prayer, in silence, in dread, in shock, in sickness, in music, in art of all sorts. But these are fleeting occasions, not typical of day-to-day experience. They recall us to an order of satisfaction and vision, which, try as we may, we cannot attain by any techniques or routines. Love comes to us, the symphonic poem brings to us, a world we feel we know very well without ever having much to do with it. It is a world given to us from we know not where; the music does it, the face of someone we love, the strange noise in the dark. And what is given is what we have wanted most, without being able to say it. That is why one is justified in coupling the divine with poetic justice or presence. The order of presence is the order of charity, the order of being present one to another.

The mystic, the religious contemplative, the true believer, see reality as truly present; the nostalgic man sees reality as if present. But the nostalgic man is not the only one who senses presence, who knows, as Proust did, that the truths of the intellect do not disclose "the idea of existence". In between the truly present and the "as if present", is the presence met in the exceptional experiences we have mentioned. Lovers are present to each other, really present; and likewise, in other confrontations, with art or nature, man is aware of the presence of something totally other than himself, not merely a direction of his field of vision. Heidegger says that "Man is only man when he is spoken to by Being. To exist is to stand within the light of Being. Only man exists in this way." And it is man only who stands within the light of presence. Man is only man when he is spoken to by some presence; until then he does not know what or who he is; he is anonymous. And the two sayings are one and the same, for presence is not the particularity of the other, but the comforting permanence of the other which signifies its Being.

We pass a strange person in the street and he or she gives us an unguarded smile; in it we know we are known, not for our reputation but for our being present. Unexpected confronting presence is like the first day of spring or the first day of summer; presence is always first, new, and with that special newness that lasts longest because it is familiar, intimate. Dostoyevsky's novels contain many of these confrontations. Sexual confrontations above all reveal presence, a world of "between" particular others, widely different others. In them the enchantingly familiar is clothed in a disconcerting physical freshness. Wherever encounters are uncorrupted by a self-concern, wherever pride and isolation are even for a second cracked by some recognition of another present, then man is permitted to visit the land of giving, mutual giving, that the king's son visited when the rose hedge parted for him.

What is so odd about the experiences that reveal presence at hand is that we are very apt to respond at first as we respond to times of dread or panic. Just as panic is the product of our feeling that all we are or care for may be taken away forever, so in love, for example, we fear that all is too good to be true and is going to be withdrawn. In panic we may approach, at least in retrospect, what we have valued but grown accustomed to. And in love we are forced to realize that what we dream is nothing to what we are offered. That is why the first effects of presence are often so bewildering. We are frightened; we tremble, we look as if we would collapse. We may even lose control, presence of mind, as another fuller presence presses on us. We yield in order to learn what this other being is like. But later, when the presence has become part of our lives, we act with more aplomb than before. This is much like what Plato had in mind when he had Aristophanes suggest, in the *Symposium*, that men are looking for their other halves in order to recover their original wholeness or fullness. We want to become one, and as Plato knew, we can do this only through love. This is another way of saying that we need to be filled in order to be ourselves. We need another half. But to make any reality one with us we must first see it as our other, not someone else's. And this is not easy, because most of the time we merely want another which we can dominate or destroy. We do not know how to live with presence.

It is difficult to view other beings as if they were permanent, when we feel we ourselves are not. Lacking dignity and stability, it is tempting to see these features in others. Why should we treat them better than ourselves? To have the kind of sight needed to see a presence, one must have had considerable practice in having presences thrown at one without developing a protective hide to bounce them off again unnoticed. Nature has given us just such a hide, in nostalgia which is unconscious, and in philosophy which is conscious. We need the second in order to confirm the purpose of the first. Nostalgia is the natural way in adversity that man has to feel his own permanence and stability, and through himself the delight in reality as a whole. It is artificial, but it is not contrived. It is second-hand, but is none the less persuasive. It is far too common to all kinds of people in all kinds of stations and situations to dismiss as unimportant.

Nostalgia combines bitterness and sweetness, the lost and the found, the far and the near, the new and the familiar, absence and presence. The past which is over and gone, from which we have been or are being removed, by some magic becomes present again for a short while. But its realness seems even more familiar, because renewed, than it ever was, more enchanting and more lovely. Magic-like it comes unasked, unanticipated, in the middle of sterility and defeat, in the middle of a waste which is impregnated with longing. And what is longed for is what we do not usually have, a sense of the intimate, immediate presentation of the whole to our consciousness. We can always know things as around us; we can know that they exist. But we seldom feel intimately attached to them. Only in experiences in which our own care goes out to meet the approaching being, do we experience reality either as whole or as present. We care for what lasts or should last. What we would give up last comes first in our caring. Since nothing looks permanent save stodgy routines, since everything is in a rush to be won or lost, the new and the lasting come to mean the same. For what refreshes jaded quests is what promises inexhaustible entertainment and concern.

What refreshes us in the fairy story—any fairy story—but the Good? Is it not the fullness of justice, the overpowering, engaging answer to our deserving or our conception of our deserving, that we respond to in myth and story, in wish and hope? And think how small the deserving can be, compared to the completeness of presence. Sleeping Beauty has so much more beauty and virtue than the prince whose character is his confidence that he need not fear to follow the call from within the castle. He has no other renown. How then had he deserved to pass where others stronger than he had perished? Perhaps the answer is that very few know for sure what is deserving and what is not. The only kind of deserving may be that which trusts in the call rather than in the person called. If this is so, no wonder we miss the deserving when we look for it in self-assurance and success. We look for it in strong men who are there only for themselves. Our strength is not our deserving, but our capacity to listen.

In moments of presence, we are made to feel that this moment is what we wanted all the time, even though we had not been able to say so. In stories of poetic justice, to which we lend our listening, all "comes right in the end". Longing is fulfilled, as we listen, and we are more than pleased. But in these stories, as in our example, The Sleeping Beauty, the emphasis is on the fulfilling rather than on the fulfilment. This is a way of saying that we must have more to do with the journey to presence than with presence itself. Partly as a result of this and partly as a result of our habitual scepticism, we wonder whether there is enough presence to guarantee all our deserving. We must not become distracted by the fulfilling to discount and minimize the fulfilment.

It is refreshing to meet a good we have wished for, even more to find it is a good already known. We are happy with what we judge good for us; we are happiest when that good is familiar. Happiness is a homecoming, and we realize this best when we think we are meeting someone or something for the first time and it turns out to be familiar. The greatest joy is a composite of familiarity and surprise. If we accept something as new, we are accepting it also as familiar, as part of the family. If we reject it, we do so because its newness is strange, unattractive because unfamiliar. What we care most for, what we take in, what we take into our home, has to belong to us already in some way. If it belongs but we do not care for it, if we are not aware of it as present, with its special presence, we see it neither as fresh nor, if we let ourselves think about it, as familiar. The only familiarity we can give full attention and approval to, is that which seems ever new, inexhaustibly fresh.

This is the context for a famous paradox that has come down to us from its religious statements by Augustine and Pascal, to T. S. Eliot's—

> "The end of all our exploring
> will be to arrive where we started
> and know the place for the first time.
> Through the unknown remembered gate."

This is the psychological equivalent of the two theological paradoxes: Augustine's "We do not say that we have found what was lost unless we recognize it", and Pascal's "Thou wouldst not seek Me, if thou didst not possess Me". The conception of happiness as a homecoming, as a return to the familiar, even the familial, assumes that there is a home to go back to, something unchanging at the back of memory which as ideal or remembered experience keeps one alive and sane. But not everyone will admit that he longs for presence or the unchanging. And not everyone will admit that happiness is a homecoming, however much his nostalgia suggests this to him.

Take that eloquent sceptic, Jacob Burckhardt, who has said: "Only the fairy-tale equates changelessness with happiness. The end of the Odyssey is so much nearer the truth. The trials of him who has suffered so much are to continue, and he must at once set out, on a grievous journey. . . . The conception of a happiness which consists in the permanence of certain conditions is of its very nature false. . . . Happiness is mere absence of pain, at best associated with a faint sense of growth."

Burckhardt had forgotten, it seems, that Odysseus's sufferings were not to continue forever, that he was to wander only until he had met people who did not know the sea. But we do not refute his scepticism merely by correcting him on this point. We would first ask whether his idea of happiness is a product of the period of isolation in the nineteenth century that he and his colleague Nietzsche lived in, a period which recognized nothing more permanent than the changing self. Or does he represent, as does Chekhov, some *fin de siècle* disillusion? While Nietzsche struggled on for a joy more positive than absence of pain, Burckhardt, admiring the greatness of the past, carefully abstained from enthusiasms for his present. We may ask also whether Burckhardt's view of happiness does not reflect the slow-down of life in the last century rather than either the self-confidence of that time or the deeper longing of the heart for a permanence he could not find. Are we to believe that "happiness is mere absence of pain" or that Burckhardt feared he could achieve no more by himself? What does he mean when he says that "happiness which consists in the permanence of certain conditions is of its very nature false"? Would he also say that no kind of changelessness would satisfy the human heart? Or was he not able to distinguish those occasions when we meet someone we can care for permanently with conditions which can be improved on? Was he too much the historian, and too timid a friend?

And yet he was right in saying that the fairy-tale concerns a changeless order, call it what you will. We could add that the fairy-tale deals with the unchanging as the familiar which renews. The Sleeping Beauty seems quite naturally to belong to the prince, and yet she is at the same time the centre of one of the least plausible stories ever told. She is at once perfectly acceptable to us as to him, and also the most magical figure of the most magical enchantment. Every story that is not immediately plausible has some enchantment, some break from the expected order. In this story alone is the enchantment so long. If there be some likeness of legend to history, one might wonder whether we too grope foolishly in the wake of an enchantment imposed by the stupidity of those who preceded us. Were we to suspect that our situation is just as opaque to normal sight, we could yearn for a new sight and an awakening. We do not know for sure our time or our rights. We experience longing, but do not know we have experienced fulfilment. We long to leave longing, to cure anguish and unease. Does fulfilment forget the longing, and the loss that made it?

What are we made for? Can we experience longing without fulfilment, fulfilment without longing? Or are we always mixed up? Does each of our serious sentiments combine absence as well as presence, sadness as well as joy? The most sensitive of men can only speak of joy or exaltation or awe by ignoring the reality of our mixed condition. The best we can hope for is for the underlying sadness to be tempered by occasions of presence. This means that we must look for a paradise that will make lasting the under-layer of all our apprehended presences, that feeling of nearness, of closeness, intimacy, to something unique and other that attends our awareness of loss as well as attention. We need not speculate or try to imagine how a man can strain his mind and feelings to take in Being. That is not within our power, and may not even be within our deepest desires. Our view of paradise must alter with our view of the inexorableness of our frailty. We cannot look forward to sunshine and songs, birds and happy glances. The blasés are right when they say: "What a bore!" We shall not have to get used to this later, to find out in heaven what heaven really is. We shall have to find out now, quickly, what we need.

Can we want, should we want, anything different from the sentiment of presence? Yes, presence itself. And will not the difference between heavenly and earthly paradises be one of intensity and quantity rather than quality? If so, then "foretaste" means much more than men think. We taste even now, in nostalgia, or in the addresses of love, a world in which reality is either with us or only just removed. Will it be different later, except much brighter, clearer, fonder, more continuous? It is the continuity of which we are now incapable. But our mixed nature we shall be wearing still so that we will not forget who we have been. If we are reborn, we shall not become different men but new men. And then we shall appreciate that paradox that the new and the lasting are one and the same. Only the new rejoices; only the lasting holds any promise. And we shall also retain a sadness to remind us that we were once mortal—and not as now to remind us that we are immortal. No longer shall we be able to pretend that we are creative, for even as we make new things (and will we?), we shall know what real creativity is. Can we conceive, do we want, a happiness that has no sadness within it? It is this very mixture of grief inside the most intense joy that is our special brand telling of both creator and his image. Is this not what we have come to understand through Pascal as "tears of joy"?

Man is happiest, not only when pain is absent or when he has a faint sense of growth, but when he is in the presence of the one he cares most for. For the religious man, the most real presence is the presence of the Lord on the altar and in men's hearts. Those who haunt men as those who haunt churches are looking for such a reality, as real as flesh and blood, in reality flesh and blood. They know that presence is both spiritual and physical, ghostly and palpable. They know it as familiar as a member of the family. The Eucharistic presence is itself a member of a holy family: father, son, and holy ghost; father, mother, and son. God came to earth as a son and brother, in family guise. He was familiar to some, strange to others. For the committed believer the real presence is an Incarnation. For the rest, who are not disillusioned with unfulfilled longing, presence, not mere absence of pain, will alone satisfy the emptiness in the soul which needs to be filled. And so they seek other incarnations, other presences in other persons, and in places, in nature, in art.

They seek in silence, and they seek intuitively. Presence tells them once they meet it, of some superiority. Someone was there before us, independent of us, waiting for us. We come into his presence, not he into ours. He will feel the same way. If we strain to show off before him, we shall miss him. If we try to control him, he will fade away. No matter how familiar and good to us, presence is elusive. Its spontaneity rebuffs all forced intimacy. In silence we are alerted to enchanted presences, to beings both familiar and new. These are the first two of the seven marks of presence: presence must be felt in silence, and felt as enchanting.[39] And it is correct to say that it must be felt. In mystical parlance the sentiment of presence is the equivalent of the metaphysical intuition of being. But it is more than equivalent, rather it is concrete and plausible. We do not get to know being until we have got in touch with it. In this special conjunction of our total self with another total being, we are aware of it through a sentiment, itself a combination of understanding and judging, rather than through some single piece of understanding, no matter how complete. The sentiment of presence is an intuition we feel, it is a judgment that reflects our understanding of its good for us. We are faced with another being that is not there before us to be looked at, analysed, controlled, but as attentive to us, at our disposal, but not to be disposed of. Its disposability is inexhaustibly in our favour if we do not try to diminish or discredit it.

When we are conscious of someone else as present, we are thinking of him as here, not beyond us, over there. To be here is to be with us, and for us. If we refuse to accept the absence of a loved one—an example Marcel often uses—if we still feel that he is here with us, feel his presence even though he has died or gone somewhere else, we can go on thinking of him as alive in some way. A belief in immortality may well arise for someone who cannot believe that when presences linger in this way, they have been obliterated. One may say that such experiences are illicit, and they may be from the point of view of either logic or physics. But from the point of view of sentiment, it is impossible to judge whether the presence felt is real or not real. Between the "idea of existence", the "sentiment of presence", and the awareness of another being, there is only a subjective shadow. Must this shadow be dispelled? Does the presence from the past, the good of the past seen and felt in nostalgia, live on only in sentiment? Could it be that these sentiments are outworks of an invisible land of permanences which we are meant to remain loyal to and even to return to? Who of us does not actually think poorly of the man who does not remain loyal to the good of the past, even if that good has apparently disappeared "for good"? If there is nothing or no one to be loyal to, how foolish to pretend attachment? Whatever the final status of the past to which we have promised to be faithful, the fact that we do keep promises can suggest that we believe in another order of reality beyond that order which, as a kaleidoscope, continually changes its pattern in front of us. That this order is a permanent one—the sense of permanence is itself a mark, the third mark, of presence—is all we need say. We should not think of presence as shifty or dissolvable because it comes to us as a subject instead of an object. It is objective enough, independent enough, even if it is as alive as we. Like us its identity, its core that defines anonymity, is to some extent beyond change. In this sense, presence or the present is really spatial. And this is why we tend to associate presence with person, body as well as soul, or a place, a land, a city, some thing.

Presence meets us concretely; it is as if it were palpable. It moves, caresses, touches us, and almost asks to be touched in return. This is but a way of saying: we caress what we care for; we are caressed by the being that cares for us. We are moved; we feel as if moved, our whole being vibrates in an encounter with another subject. And yet palpable as presence seems, it is not primarily material. Why do lovers like the dark, twilight, soft lights? Not only because they achieve privacy, but also because their bodies do not there obtrude to the point of driving away a sense of the spirit that moves the flesh. What is the special appeal of ballet but its exhibit of spirit revealing itself when flesh is moving but silent? And yet presence is the permanence of concrete being, of spirit that must be incarnate. Just as the disciple Thomas had to touch the resurrected Jesus in order to believe, so now the religious man eats the Body of Christ for his salvation. For others presence spells the nearness which inspires touching. What is "just there" hardly affects or moves us, because it does not touch us, and we do not touch it. It is not intended to be in place for us personally, but exists separately, indifferent to us. To live in an atmosphere of presence is to have escaped an indifferent universe.

What do we mean when we say that we are touched or moved? Do we not mean that we are in the presence of someone or something which speaks to what is permanent in us? We touch the hand of someone else and feel the whole person. But we have to be little used to touching or else the touching must be unexpected, if we are to feel the person through the body, and not just the body. So important is touching sometimes that we hold back until we have accumulated beforehand the full expectation of the surprise that must accompany the familiarity. Touching, like a handshake, is merely the overture to what may turn into dialogue or communion. When our aching overflows, we caress, we reach out and put a hand on our son's head or on our wife's cheek.

From these slight gestures of presence to the density of *Wuthering Heights* the distance is small and is usually travelled in secret. Most of us do not disclose our privacy, and our sentiment of presence lies safely at its centre. We do not disclose our grief and our creativity as readily as we show our vices and our passions. And these are what we are led to notice first in Heathcliffe. Only secondly do we see that he is turbulent just because his entire being is filled with the presence of someone else. "Her presence was with me; it remained while I refilled the grave, and led me home—I could almost see her, and yet I could not! I ought to have sweat blood then, from the anguish of my yearning—from the fervour of my supplications to have but one glimpse." Or: "I cannot look down to this floor, but her features are shaped on the flags! In every cloud, in every tree—filling the air by night, and caught by glimpses in every object by day—I am surrounded with her image! The most ordinary faces of men and women—my own features—mock me with a resemblance. The entire world is a dreadful collection of memoranda that she did exist and that I have lost her." But is this not just what he cannot accept? *Wuthering Heights* is charged with presences, alive and dead. On the surface one notices love and hate, and both are greater than in the average story of love or revenge, because they last longer. Both love and hate are eternal, they stretch in their terrestrial longings beyond the flesh. For it is not the flesh or the spirit which is adored and despised; it is their being-together, in Cathy and Heathcliffe. And you cannot dissolve them, not even death can, until the lovers are joined. Cathy will not rest; her cold hand bleeds on the window's jagged edge as Lockwood grasps it; she does not rot thirteen years after her death; she waits for her other half to die. She can no more die without him than he can live without her.

Being moved is the fourth mark of presence. In silence we are moved by something abiding which we feel to be both familiar and unexpected. We are moved—and this is what distinguishes the sentiment of presence from sentimentality—not by ourselves but by another being moving into the area of our presence. We do not move ourselves, save in that comic pantomime called sentimentality; we are moved by someone else presenting himself to us. This is the fifth mark of presence, presence as a present. When someone else gives himself to us, puts himself at our disposal, we are moved, first to gratitude and then to communion, later to a presentation of all our loyalty.

"To be incapable of presence is to be in some manner not only occupied but encumbered with one's own self", and "each of us becomes the centre of a sort of mental space arranged in concentric zones of decreasing interest and participation" (Marcel). He who is not present to others, because of his egocentricity, is likely not to be present to himself either. It is possible, and the Renaissance bears us out, for reflectiveness and practicality to live together at high pitch in one nature. More often one finds that the reflective man—now called introverted—is considered less a man than the man of affairs. But the latter may be, morally speaking, more egocentric than the former. He may merely regard nature and society as fields for self-aggrandisement. Such a man knows nothing of self-mastery for the sake of something greater than himself. Like the more innocent absent-minded, or uncollected, person, he cannot be trusted to do what does not suit his own interest. He is incapable of keeping promises or of achieving genuine intimacy with anybody or anything. He has no standards of assurance or any knowledge to permit him to ignore either the nature of things, or specific realities. He fears them all and feels neither responsibility nor presence of mind that would make him invulnerable. He is an alien to straightforward talk and actions. He should, therefore, feel like a foreigner among men. And if he sometimes does feel that he does not belong anywhere, he may feel also that there should be a place where he can belong. He suspects others of not caring for him; he suspects they will not mention him after he has left, except to speak ill of him. And yet his own presence does not linger. Nor can he predict how he will treat others, even his wife and children. Despite his power for getting and keeping what belongs to others, he does not have even himself under control. These are the symptoms of an alien, of a morally anonymous man.

The only adequate cure for anonymity is the gift of presence. Presence is silent; it encourages communion; it makes one open to all the scents of interpretation. It is beyond anxiety, patiently awaiting our call. No doubt of that: we have to call presence, invoke it, as Marcel says. We cannot only wait. But even so, it comes in its own time which becomes our time—or, in "no time at all"—bringing gifts. Presence is not our time. Our time is anxiety, either guilty or fearful of the future. We have to be given a present, and through or by means of this present we participate in eternity of some sort. The present does not belong to us; it cannot even abide with us unless we are both strong and whole. To be humble is not enough, to make an effort is not enough either. You have to long for the gift of presence. Few people know what this means except in some religious terms. But their religion has so little effect on their lives, and they are usually unable to understand that you do not have to be a "Christian" to know you need presence. Prayer is itself a longing for presence. But there are other longings too, which are answered by presences. We are not human because we can triumph over time—on the contrary, we are always victims of time, to the end, to death. We are human because we can, by longing as by prayer, have something to do with the gifts of presence: beauty and justice.

It is not enough to speak of presence as the being invoked by prayer and longing: we must say more. "Presence invokes a reciprocity" of caring. We care for those who take care of us.

We take care of those who may care for us. Both prayer and longing are caring directed away from the self to a presence which we hope can be at our disposal. Presence is a gift, and we receive it as a gift, with love beforehand and gratitude after. Presence is a favour granted us, a recognition, a compassion, a pity for our own insufficiency and our deserving. It is also our piety, our devotion, and our thanks. When Pascal talks of the order of charity, he is talking of a reciprocal order of divine gift and divinely inspired human practice. And it is pertinent to learn that "charity" comes from the Greek χάρις which is translated in the English New Testament as grace. The order of charity is the order of grace; the grace, which when accepted by man brings both charity or love (ἀγάπη) and charm (χάρισμα), is the gift from another across an apparent abyss. It is that package of the familiar and the unexpected that so enlarges the topography of the self.

Presence is a gift, but not a random one. Presence is given from design to a you. Presence is caring. It is also the effect of caring, the natural and the spontaneous effect of caressing, charm, and devotion. And the more devoted, the more charming, the more full of grace, the greater the gift, the greater the thanks and the fullness of grace (χαῖρε, κεχαριτωμένη: Hail, full of grace!). One gives thanks for the gift one has not fully deserved, which one is surprised into receiving. One accepts the gift as due, because it seems so familiar or longed for. And there too is the enchantment of the world of presence or poetic justice, the world where things come out all right in the end. We are enchanted because we are both mystified and charmed, because we are encountering mystery and charm, the unexpected and incomprehensible on the one hand, and on the other that which belongs to us. The sixth mark of presence is caring, which is mysterious and charismatic.

We are refreshed and renewed by the story of The Sleeping Beauty, and not least because it is a story of renewal. And this is the answer when we are asked what its charm is. The charm or enchantment lies not in prince or princess, in castle or thorn hedge, or even in cook and cook's boy, but in the telling of an order that awaits a touch to be reawakened. There is grace of every kind in fairy tales; in the fairy godmothers, the wise old women (the χάριτες, as the Greeks say), in their promises and their gifts, in the slumbering of gifts in magic, in the re-awakening, the all-caring tune of the finale. There is promise and betrayal, longing and recovery. The tale records encounters between two worlds, the world of probability which makes us slumber, the world of presence which makes us wonder. The tale records a reception of gifts no man can completely deserve. The tale transports us willingly to the field of poetic justice, where life is right and ordered. But is this also the order of probability? By no means. For the order of probability, which is the order of all the unrest we know so well, lacks the fullness that presence gives.

And this is the final mark of presence itself, fullness. Of the seven marks of presence, six lead up to fullness, for this is what everyone longs to have. And the other marks are the conditions of its achievement. Only in experiences of justice and presence is life complete; only when the sense of completeness is at the same time enlivening and enlightening is man happy. Repleteness does not satisfy; not only is it enervating, it is the fatigue after the battle, the threshold to further unrest. The occasional victories of deserving do not convince us, for they are offset by defeats as numerous. Will we only be convinced of the inevitability of justice if we see unassailable evidence of a world of fullness? Without a doubt. So the question we began with we return to: what kind of evidence can we accept as unassailable? The answer is, I think, certain, but is also elusive because it lies outside our normal sense of caution. It is that we visit the order of poetic justice every time we are in the presence of a fullness we care for: in love, in longing, in compassion, in justice, in art, in liturgy, in prayer, in nature, in suffering, in silence, in thinking. Our cagey world is bordered by a galaxy of such opportunities to advance from fear and probability, from isolation and unease, to the immeasurable spheres of fullness and grace. "And of this fullness have we all received, and grace for grace" (John I, 16). We do not need to believe in Christ or to be even normally religious, to understand that this fullness and this grace which the Gospel mentions addresses itself specifically to a theory of experience that has advanced beyond both banality and tragedy into the human quest for the completeness that feels permanent.

The story of The Sleeping Beauty need not, perhaps had better not, be read as religious allegory. Whatever likeness we have illumined is, in a way, very arbitrary and personal. And yet, if the story continues to make refreshing sense to young and old alike, are we not justified in groping as far as we can for the roots of our spontaneous, unreflective response to it? If so, is it equally permissible to suggest that this is a story of the fullness of time, and that the fullness of time reminds one that "when the fullness of time was come, God sent forth his son . . . to redeem them that were under the Law"?[40] But in what sense? Surely, at the very least, in the philosophical sense of the reawakening and restoring of the beauty and justice that had been slumbering. Is this not the clear context of the most simple experiences of presence? In the fullness of time—and no man knows the day or the hour—we are awakened by a line of music—no matter how banal—or by a smile from a stranger, to the conviction that we have been waiting on the wrong side of a thorn hedge, that the area surrounding the castle is so much larger and more delightful than the area outside the hedge, but that we can cross it into the castle in no time at all. In a land where all is given and nothing grasped, where piety is aroused by compassion, where longing meets fullness, man decisively enters the order of poetic justice. Every man enters it whether he is educated to know it or not. And even a man who does know it does not always know it well enough to communicate it to others. That is why it is good to read and even philosophize about the story of The Sleeping Beauty. Experience teaches man much, poetry even more, and philosophy confirms as it reflects on both.

III

EPILOGUE

For all those whose experience has led them through times of waste, alienation, and emptiness, the ideal of presence, with its principal characteristic, fullness, will seem the obvious end to seek. To those who are satisfied with what life has brought them, there is nothing for us to say. But these are few indeed. He who is empty would be filled. He who is divided from place or person would be reunited. He who has seen his efforts wasted through little fault of his own, would have his deserving recognized. For all those whose experiences have discouraged them from rejoicing in their gifts, stories of poetic justice can, at least, distract them from an irrational world. Nothing could be more rational than for effort to be rewarded, and yet nothing, apparently, is less to be counted on than that the world is arranged that justice be done.

There have been times in history when men believed, in one way or another, that justice is done sooner or later. This is the heart of religious hope. It is also, more immediately, the faith in progress of the nineteenth century. But this faith was the product of a successful class rather than of humanity as a whole, and already has had to be modified after the dreadful inhumanity and injustice of the last thirty-five years. To-day only those who are personally untouched by rage and grief can say without insulting the innocents and the martyrs, that the world is so arranged that justice will be done. Those whose lives were wasted by other men's inhumanity cannot be helped. Those who remain owe it to themselves to arrange the world so that such inhumanity may at least be diminished.

But to lessen injustice is still not to assure posterity of a world which will be characterized simply by its justice and a fullness of life for each person born into it. One would have to be excessively simple-minded, or a politician, to imagine such a future. For in the future as in the present, stories of poetic justice will be needed to encourage persons who cannot see in their lives the fullness they need and almost deserve. In the future as well as at present, such fairy stories as that of The Sleeping Beauty will be read as a holiday from worry and suspense, as illustrations of the proper relation between deserving and fulfilment. In this story of reawakening of a lost beauty, a return to life of all that makes life worth having, men, women, and children will continue to recognize the ideal they are familiar with through longing. There is no deeper longing, and no wish more suited to the contemporary scene, than the longing to recognize and be recognized, the longing for fulfilment through recognition. And there is no more fitting presentation of this fulfilment than in the awakening of a beautiful girl by a noble young man. This is how life can be fulfilled. It is, at least, the beginning of fulfilment. From the lofty vantage of this happy recognition scene, how distant and harmless seems the viciousness of the way of the world. Wherever beauty is reawakened, the brutality and the snubs of man to man, as well as the pressures of acceleration and quantity, look so small as to appear almost comic. That men are indifferent to other men, that the world they admire or cravenly support, also is indifferent to persons, seems itself only a story to anyone who has just been recognized for the person he is.

In his encounters with other persons, other presences, man loses his frightening anonymity. And as his namelessness is repaired, so he sees the possibility of a full return, to the dimly conceived home of occasional moments of nostalgia. But a full return home opens up the greatest question of all, the question of the whereabouts of home itself. Has modern man been made so homeless, perhaps, that he cannot conceive even homelessness adequately until it has been reduced to something smaller and more comprehensible, such as anonymity? To understand that one is homeless, one must believe in home. But it is easier to be anonymous and to remember that one has a name others are not interested in. And so we think that the restoration of one's name through the recognition of some presence near one, is but the beginning of a restoration to the health that can flourish only in the atmosphere of home. Not until a man is named again, will he have the courage to believe in and look for the home he has lost. That there is such a home and paradise no one can doubt who has encountered and been recognized by some beautiful presence.

NOTES

THESE notes are added so that the reader can explore, if he wishes, more leisurely the implications of ideas only touched on so far, and so that he may come to realize how extensive is the contemporary reflection on these matters.

1. Page 11. The detective story, the Western, the romantic story of love or adventure.
2. Page 11. First published in 1812.
3. Page 11. "The folk-tale is the primer of the picture language of the soul. . . . Its world of magic is symptomatic of fevers deeply burning in the psyche: permanent presences, desires, fears."—JOSEPH CAMPBELL.
4. Page 12. "The content of folklore is metaphysics. Our inability to see this is due to our abysmal ignorance of metaphysics and its technical terms."—ANANDA COOMARASWAMY.
5. Page 12. One may even deserve evil, loss as well as good, and one may be rewarded with a presence lacking caring. This is the product of an initial carelessness or base evaluation. See W. W. Jacobs's story *The Monkey's Paw*, which Mr. John L. Sweeney has drawn to my attention. Poetic justice is given, not earned. And yet can we believe anyone is given it who has not earned it?
6. Page 13. Grimm's name for the tale we call in English *The Sleeping Beauty*, was *Dornröschen*. In French it is *La Belle au Bois Dormant*. It is worth quoting Mr. Campbell's paragraph on this tale from his book, *The Hero with a Thousand Faces*: "The Lady of the House of Sleep is a familiar figure in fairy tale and myth. We have already spoken of her, under the forms of Brynhild and little Briar-rose. She is the paragon of all paragons of beauty, the reply to all desire, the bliss-bestowing goal of every hero's earthly and unearthly quest. She is mother, sister, mistress, bride. Whatever in the world has lured, whatever has seemed to promise joy, has been premonitory of her existence—in the deep of sleep, if not in the cities and forests of the world. For she is the incarnation of the promise of perfection; the soul's assurance that, at the conclusion of its exile in a world of organized inadequacies, the bliss that once was known will be known again: the comforting, the nourishing, the 'good' mother—young and beautiful—who was known to us and even tasted, in the remotest past. Time sealed her away, yet she is dwelling still, like one who sleeps in timelessness, at the bottom of the timeless sea."
7. Page 13. Wilhelm and Jacob Grimm were collecting the tales all through the Napoleonic Wars. The first English translation, that of Edgar Taylor, was made in 1823, when folk tales and ballads had hardly survived the worldly confidence and commonsense of the 18th century, when the new pressures of life in the 19th century could not be satisfied by 18th-century complacency.
8. Page 15. On the mortal combat between man's technical powers and his sense of mystery, the personal and the imaginative, Gabriel Marcel

has had more to say than anyone else. See especially his *Being and Having*; *The Mystery of Being*, Vol. I; and *L'Homme contre l'Humain*. See also Edwin Muir's "The Decline of the Imagination", *The Listener*, May 10, 1951.

9. Page 16. See the interesting series of books on false utopias, from Aldous Huxley's *Brave New World* to Koestler's *Darkness at Noon*, Orwell's *Animal Farm* and *Nineteen Eighty-Four*, and Virgil Gheorghiu's *The Twenty-Fifth Hour*.

10. Page 16. See the essay "Mass and Person" by J. M. Domenach and Paul Ricoeur, *Cross Currents*, Winter 1952.

11. Page 16. This was first remarked on in 1859 by John Stuart Mill with a clarity that has not been exceeded since.

12. Page 16. See Henry Adams's chapter on acceleration in history in *The Education of Henry Adams*. Adams did not foresee at the beginning of the century that this acceleration might overwhelm man's capacity to keep up with it. His attitude towards this was self-consciously detached. The best account of this complexity or "agglomeration" or "plenitude" is still Ortega's *The Revolt of the Masses*, written in 1930.

13. Page 18. Modern man is not in search of a soul, as Jung put it, but in search of his home. Or is it more correct to say that in searching for his home he finds his soul? So Augustine believed, and eventually one has to choose between him and Proust. One way to decide with Proust is to decide that there is no real alternative anyway.

14. Page 18. In his essay, "Marcel Proust", in *The Atlantic Monthly*, Oct., 1948, Professor Harry Levin makes the interesting observation that Proust's "figure in the carpet" was non-recognition or "the failure of his worldly characters to recognize the claims of human decency, the cut that the narrator meets from his best friend, Saint-Loup. This is a negative criterion, based upon values whose absence is profoundly felt, but attached to a mode of existence which expects very little to happen." Non-recognition in Proust means at this level the failure to see and be loyal to either human values or human persons. Proust's cult of friendship was one way he had of righting this balance. But non-recognition means loss as well as the "cut", and it was the loss of the past with all that Proust loved and lived that his writing aimed to recover, through recognition, through prolonged nostalgia of the writer's art. Proust was the first to register the great thematic change from 19th to 20th century: from voluntary isolation to non-recognition (from "outsider" to "prisoner", as Mr. Martin Turnell has so succinctly put it). In his great work both levels of recognition are brought forth and harmonized, the moral and the psychological, the problem of friendship and nostalgia. It should be said that his work was conceived and, in the rough, completed by 1912. Only one step beyond Proust and his understanding of the lost paradise must one go to link anonymity, longing, and homelessness specifically with recognition (fidelity) and nostalgia. Gabriel Marcel began to take this step in the early thirties in his second metaphysical journal, *Being and Having*, but he has tended to concentrate on the moral aspects of non-recognition rather than on the more subjective reality of homelessness and nostalgia.

15. Page 19. See Marcel's remark in the epilogue to his *Rome n'est plus dans Rome*, 1951, on the death of stoicism.

16. Page 19. Simone Weil has done much, in her *Attente de Dieu*, to clarify the difference between the two experiences which the two words "suffering" and "affliction" can be made to distinguish. For example: "In the realm of suffering, affliction is something apart, specific and irreducible. It is quite a different thing from simple suffering. It takes possession of the soul and marks it through and through with its own particular mark, the mark of slavery."

17. Page 20. And yet Kierkegaard could say: "If we lacked nothing, we should not be overcome with homesickness. . . . This impertinent inquietude, this holy hypochondria."

18. Page 20. This view is most persuasively given by Miss Elizabeth Bowen in "The Cult of Nostalgia", *The Listener*, Aug. 9, 1951. She admits that "a very great part of the writing of our own period has served as a carrier—yes, a promoter too—of this nostalgia", and she hopes that nostalgia may now be declining. Why? Because the nostalgics do not have the vitality and youth needed to grasp "the unfamiliar, the unforeseen relation between things, the breakthrough of an unexpected light, the new experience". They find the world "less habitable than it used to be" and sacrifice the quest for "the present, the 'now', the moment" to the illusion of remembrance. And even though she understands that "our emotions, even our senses seek something stable to cling to . . . in some form, an abiding city", she prefers the attitude of youth, of "blind vitality", of "barbarian energy", which can "take its moments straight". If the period we are now going through is only a valley of despond between two peaks of confidence and humaneness—a view suspiciously wishful—nostalgia could then be regarded as having only a holding function. But if men continue to be cut off from both quiet and decency, then nostalgia could be a saving rather than a holding sentiment. Furthermore, Miss Bowen's easy mention of youth, as against grey middle-age, taking its moments straight, raises the Proustian question again as to how effectively men have ever been able to live in the present. The present, the now, the moment, are not necessarily one and the same. It is tempting to add that the great illusion of the twenties was that men could live in the moment and be happy. No doubt there is sane truth in this illusion, but Miss Bowen has helped suppress it by not recognizing the connection between nostalgia and the present.

Miss Bowen's talk was printed in an issue of *The Listener* which included an editorial, "Homesickness", in which the editorial writer sought to correct the one-sided view of Miss Bowen. He said, in part: "Nostalgia or homesickness is a deep-seated emotion in the human make-up. . . . There is a school of thought that interprets the saga of Odysseus in psychological terms and sees in it the longing which a traveller carries in his heart to go back to his own place. . . ." *The Odyssey* is, it is true, a story of a homecoming, and certainly worth reading carefully for psychological lore. It is right to remark here that this homecoming ends with an account of manifold recognitions almost as severe as the ordeals of the voyaging itself. Odysseus could not stop wandering even after he returned home until the oar, the symbol of this wandering, looked like something that did not connote exile, namely, the winnowing fan.

19. Page 20. Pliny's line recalls T. S. Eliot's "Home is where we start from".

20. Page 20. For we are "exiled children of Eve" (from the *Salve Regina*).

21. Page 20. This word is crucial in human life. Heidegger has spoken of man as a "Wesen der Ferne", a creature of distance, a being who can transcend or surpass himself. Whatever meaning one gives to transcendence, whether it be "vertical" or "horizontal", to use Father Copleston's distinction, whether it be epistemological or religious, there is also the fact of man's being distanced as well as distancing. When he feels himself distant from home, persons, values, distance comes to mean alienation, and then man, instead of surpassing, becomes surpassed or even superseded.

22. Page 20. Nostalgia is: "That feeling took possession of heart which is unequalled as well for sweetness as for bitterness—the feeling of lively regret for vanished youth, for once familiar happiness." Turgenev. "It is the sound of little things that comes down out of the short past and shatters me. The sound of skates in the winter air, the whine of the north-easter, the marrow-piercing cry of kingfishers over deserted meadows. . . . Are they merely the tender trivialities of one man's recollection, or are they eternal things? . . . They are very dear to me and I am frightened of the answer." H. E. Bates. "The permanent essence of things, usually concealed, is set free and our true self awakes, takes on fresh life." We "cease to feel mediocre, accidental, mortal", because we have by-passed "the inexorable law which decrees that only that which is absent can be imagined". Imagination lacks "the idea of existence". It is the "idea of existence" as Proust calls it that Marcel and others have since called "presence".

23. Page 21. No one in this century was more successfully a part of the world he lived in than John Buchan. And yet he combined in himself, as he knew, the nineteenth century beliefs in individual effort and friendship with the knowledge that he was living in a world in which these things could be foiled at a moment's notice. His autobiography is frankly nostalgic and in this is different from most autobiographies written before it. Buchan knew that the past was not inferior to the present, and that the present could not make up for the past, and he did not shrink from expressing his nostalgia for specific times, places, and people. But in this he does differ from many since who are not able to feel any nostalgia for particular scenes and persons of their own past, but whose nostalgia evokes and is evoked by the artificial scenes of literature and hasty travel. For the latter there is a nostalgic note of this kind in their reading of Buchan's more normal remark that "if paradise be a renewal of what was happy and innocent in our earthly days, mine will be some such golden afternoon within sight and sound of Tweed". Nostalgia to-day tends to become more spiritual and at the same time harder to fulfil. There are still two kinds of nostalgia, however, each reflecting a different stage in the strange 20th century: the longing to be somewhere else, and the longing merely to be elsewhere.

24. Page 22. Nostalgia "suddenly brings us a breath of fresh air, refreshing just because we have breathed it once before—of that purer air which the poets have vainly tried to establish in paradise, whereas it could not convey that profound sensation of renewal if it had not already been breathed, for the only true paradise is the paradise that we have lost." Jacques Maritain has said that "to be written as it should be written the work of a Proust needs the inner light of a St. Augustine". This may or may not be. The parallel between them is, nevertheless, striking.

Both were concerned with disquietude, memory, time; both were searching for an abiding city, the lost paradise. Proust could not believe that there is an abiding city that we have not in some measure already experienced between birth and death; he did not believe in personal immortality. Augustine, on the contrary, did believe, and his reply to Proust's saying that the only paradise is the lost paradise, would have been: "We have no fear that there should be no place of return, merely because by our own act we fell from it: our absence does not cause our home to fall, which is Thy Eternity."

If Proust's category was non-recognition, it may be said that Augustine's was recognition. We know because we have known; we know because we are known. For what Augustine, and not Proust, had known was eternity, not just the past. And Proust could not be quieted by the knowledge that he was already known, by friends and loving relations. He was obsessed by time, by loss, by the inability of others to understand him or anyone completely. Belonging superficially only to the Christian world, he belonged profoundly to the twentieth century world in which God is dead. He wished to keep what he had, by recognizing the past in a fullness he had not realized. This involved not recognition as much as recovery, a special kind of return. Augustine too returned, but in a different dimension, through a mutual recognition of the divine and himself. There is a sense in which no recovery of the transient, however nostalgically, or artistically arranged, can yield the moral and psychological stability which the soul looks for in recognition. Proust returned only to himself; Augustine, at least as he understood it, to another land altogether to which he had access through memory. As Georges Poulet has said in his fascinating *Etudes sur le temps humain*: "In Proustian thought memory plays the same supernatural role that grace does in Christian thought." It is interesting to note that while Proust's disquietude is temporal, concerned with loss of self and others, with death, Augustine's is spatial. Augustine felt he had not found the "way". His besetting problem was "waywardness", his life a voyage to the city of God. "I wandered afar but I remembered Thee. I heard Thy voice behind me calling me to return, but I could scarcely hear it for the tumult of my unquieted passions." Both men depended much on their mothers, but Augustine far more than Proust. Augustine's dependence on his mother was less sentimental but of closer import because he always knew she was in touch with the living eternity he himself was seeking. Proust's mother had nothing but herself to give, and that was not enough to relieve his loneliness.

25. Page 22. There is no older notion in Western civilization than of man as a voyager, either as a pilgrim to home or heaven or, the reverse, as a wanderer or exile. It is also at the centre of Homer; it is in the Greek tragic dramas; it is in Plato. It is especially Jewish and Christian. In our own time it is revived in the writings of Joyce and Kafka. Marcel has called one of his collections of essays *Homo Viator*, and he has justified this by saying that human life is spatial and life unavoidably a voyage. It may be said that human life is also temporal, and, as Proust understood, life unavoidably a return. These two aspects are obviously intertwined. The concept of presence itself combines both space and time, for presence makes itself felt somewhere, coming from an elsewhere, and it makes itself felt in the middle of time.

26. Page 23. Restless, we are blind, nostalgic, and we have a chance to see. In ordinary disquietude, we do not know what is wrong, what is missing.

27. Page 24. There are two texts relating to this which deserve to be placed side by side: one by Pascal, the other by Emil Brunner. The first is *Pensée 172*: "We do not rest satisfied with the present. We anticipate the future as too slow in coming, as if in order to hasten its course; or we recall the past, to stop its too rapid flight. . . . For the present is generally painful to us. . . . Let each one examine his thoughts, and he will find them all occupied with the past and the future. We scarcely ever think of the present. . . . The present is never our end. The past and the present are our means, the future alone is our end. So we never live, but we hope to live; and, as we are always preparing to be happy, it is inevitable we should never be so." In his essay, "The Christian Sense of Time", *Cross Currents*, Fall 1950, Brunner has said: "Sinful man is a being for whom a true present is intended but who does not have it because he is always vainly occupied in past and future, but never in the present. It would be worth the trouble to analyse more exactly the psychological manifestation of this private existence of the present." One of the aims of these notes is, of course, to do just that. But it would be wrong to isolate the psychological aspect of presence from the other aspects, from the need for justice, and from nostalgia. What is needed more than anything else to-day is an approach to these problems which comprehends them thematically and historically. To do this involves, unfortunately, some sacrifice of rhetorical and systematic neatness.

28. Page 24. Both Marcel and Buber were writing of "the present" and "presence" in 1923. The pioneer texts are: Buber's *I and Thou*, especially pp.10–13, 106–111, and Marcel's *Metaphysical Diary*, pp. 266, 289. Marcel even discusses Proust and exile from home, on p. 259. It was used by Father Joseph Maréchal S.J. in his *Etudes sur la Psychologie des Mystiques*, 1924, as "le sentiment de présence," which is the central fact of mystical states. It is the same sentiment of presence that makes a person aware of ghosts, psychical presences. In 1933 Marcel wrote his important essay, "On the Ontological Mystery", in which he summed up his thinking of the preceding years on the moral and metaphysical implications of presence. A year later Professor Louis Lavelle's *La Présence Totale* came out, in which without any reference to anyone else, he sketched the epistemological and metaphysical aspects of presence, in many details overlapping Marcel. Martin Buber's distinction of I and Thou, which Marcel has made use of for many years, and his notion of a "between" in dialogue, depend on an idea of presence. More recently Emil Brunner, in the essay mentioned above, has, without any allusion to Marcel, discussed the moral and theological aspects of presence in terms almost identical with those Marcel and Buber use. For example: "Sinful man, not present in the sense we have explained, experiences this non-presence above all in his relations with other men. In effect, he is not there for them. Sinful man is too occupied with his own past and his own future to realize truly the Thou of another. He searches for himself because he does not possess his life as present. That which morally is called the lack of charity might be called metaphysically under the aspect of existence in time—the fact of not being there for others. . . .

Notes

He who is united to Christ in faith enters into a new relation with other men . . . man suddenly has time for his neighbour. . . . He is present for him, and in this presence he has himself the experience of the true present . . . etc."

29. Page 24. Lavelle holds that "the initial experience" is always "the experience of the presence of being", and he says that "the task of philosophical thought is to attach oneself to this essential experience". By this one can see how far away are the other contemporary notions of philosophizing, especially that which holds that philosophy is puzzle solving.

30. Page 25. For Lavelle consciousness itself is "a dialogue with being". "The presence of being creates our proper intimacy with being." "The sentiment of presence is the experience of the whole." So paradoxically it is through the individual, the concrete, the simple, that the whole is taken in. "Being cannot be distinguished from universal intimacy." The language of metaphysics and epistemology borrows from the language of persons. This is the natural order, the existential order, in which a human being approaches the whole.

31. Page 25. "The present is the fundamental character of being." "Presence is concrete eternity." Lavelle.

32. Page 26. See note 27 for Brunner's moral interpretation of presence as charity.

33. Page 26. "It is not the presence of being that we invoke but our presence to being." "Presence is not conferred on being by the *I* but on the *I* by being." "Every particular presence is mutual, but is based on the absolute presence of the whole." For Marcel too, as Lavelle in the preceding quoted sentences, presence is invoked or refused; it is when active a giving of the self, or a giving of some being to the self; it is, in his language, "availability", which is a more active form of what Lavelle calls "intimacy". With the tale of The Sleeping Beauty in mind, it is interesting to read in Marcel that "a presence can only be invoked or evoked, the evocation being fundamentally and essentially magical".

34. Page 26. Lavelle seems to use Proustian terminology in his chapter headings: "La Présence Dispersée" and "La Présence Retrouvée". He is testifying to the dispersal, especially in contemporary life, of the sense of presences, through which man senses the whole. In his "meditation", "The Field Path", Heidegger has recently (1950) taken up the same theme. "The simple things enshrine the mystery of the enduring and the great." He too says that man has become distracted and lost his way, "bored by simple things". "The simple things have taken flight. Their silent power has withered away."

35. Page 29. "Little Briar Rose," *Grimm's Fairy Tales*, translated by Margaret Hunt, Pantheon Books, New York.
   The typographical arrangement is by my friend, Mr. Morton Bradley, Jr.

36. Page 101. "I live like a foreigner who has become assimilated to a country not his own; I am liked by the natives and I like them in turn . . . but I know that I am a foreigner and in secret I regret the fields of my homeland. . . . Where is my homeland? I shall not see it, I shall die in a foreign land. And sometimes I so passionately long for it! . . .

But just as a stranger in a foreign land sometimes recognizes, with emotion, his homeland in the odor of a flower or the hue of a sunset, so I even here feel the beauty and freshness of the promised world. I feel it in the fields and in the woods, in the song of the birds and in the peasant following his plow, in the eyes of children and sometimes in their words, in the divinely kind smiles of women, in the sympathy of man for man, in sincere and universal simplicity, in an occasional word that glows or an unexpected line of poetry which pierces the darkness like a flash of lightning, and in many other things—especially in suffering." M. O. Gershenzon, "A Correspondence between Two Corners", *Partisan Review*, Sept., 1948.

37. Page 102. C. S. Lewis's *The Weight of Glory*.

And also H. E. Bates's: "This piece of country creates in me the restless impression that I have lived in it before. This feeling, though I was born and brought up a hundred and fifty miles away, becomes very strong in late August. It is a feeling of dreamy disquietude, a strong feeling that an experience out of the past remains unfinished and that now some new journey, a day by the sea, an hour or two on the wide marshlands, will bring it to completion."

38. Page 111. Max Picard's *The World of Silence*.

39. Page 122. Stendhal's fascination for the unexpected is always a respect for the active, novel, even foolish. His real grasp of presence is not in the unexpected but in the quiet of nature, as in Fabrizio's reverie over the panorama of Como and the Alps or Julien's survey of the country around Verrières from a hilltop. In such lofty and silent situations, Stendhal felt peace. The unexpected, "imprévu", is, in practice at least, only a political antithesis to the mediocrity of his time. His unexpected situations are always risky and even catastrophic. When the unexpected is divorced from the familiar, as in Stendhal, the impact of it is not enchanting, merely shocking.

40. Page 130. In "Eternity is the fullness of time—that word taken in the sense in which it is used where it is said that Christ came in the fullness of time." Kierkegaard, *Journals*, page 74.

Cowley Publications is a work of the Society of St. John the Evangelist, a religious community for men in the Episcopal Church. The books we publish are a significant part of our ministry, together with the work of preaching, spiritual direction, and hospitality. Our aim is to provide books that will enrich their readers' religious experience and challenge it with fresh approaches to religious concerns.